ICE

Why I Was Born to Score

George Gervin
with Scoop Jackson

TRIUMPH
BOOKS

Library of Congress Cataloging-in-Publication Data

Names : Gervin, George, author. | Jackson, Robert, author.
Title : Ice : why I was born to score / George Gervin, with Robert Scoop Jackson.
Description : Chicago, Illinois : Triumph Books LLC, [2023] |
Identifiers : LCCN 2023009656 | ISBN 9781637272312 (cloth)
Subjects : LCSH : Gervin, George. | African American basketball players—United States—Biography. | Basketball players—United States—Biography. | African American basketball coaches—United States—Biography. | Basketball coaches—United States—Biography. | San Antonio Spurs (Basketball team)—History. | National Basketball Association—History. | BISAC : SPORTS & RECREATION / Basketball | SPORTS & RECREATION / Cultural & Social Aspects
Classification : LCC GV884.G47 A3 2023 | DDC 796.323092 [B]—dc23/eng/20230310
LC record available at https://lccn.loc.gov/2023009656

This book is available in quantity at special discounts for your group or organization. For further information, contact:

Triumph Books LLC
814 North Franklin Street
Chicago, Illinois 60610
(312) 337-0747
www.triumphbooks.com

Printed in U.S.A.
ISBN: 978-1-63727-231-2
Design by Nord Compo

"All Scripture is inspired of God and beneficial for teaching, for reproving, for setting things straight, for disciplining in righteousness, so that the man of God may be fully competent, completely equipped for every good work."

—2 Timothy 3:16-17

CONTENTS

FOREWORD

He's a legend.

When I was around 10 or 11 years old, I remember the older people coming around, comparing me to this dude they kept calling "Ice" or "Iceman." And I never knew who he was because I was watching games in that Kobe Bryant, Michael Jordan, Shaquille O'Neal era of basketball. As a kid I needed to find out who this guy was. And once I did my research, I immediately saw the similarities and I really appreciated his old-school style of play. It drove me a bit. Watching this guy at my size be successful gave me incentive to keep pushing and keep going. He was one of those few players I could directly relate to. Just seeing someone who could more around the court and who was my size gave me confidence.

It was hard at times for me looking for inspiration in people who looked like I did and played like I played because coming up we were taught that basketball was a strong man's game. At my height you had to be able to bully somebody in the post. But George played with a finesse that made me feel comfortable playing the way I did. It was just reassurance for me. I always knew what I wanted to be, but seeing someone who looked like me play the game at the highest level just made my dreams more attainable.

Now, I was too young to have actually seen him play. All I heard were the stories, but going back and researching; really seeing who the greats were while I was trying to find myself and find my place in the game; seeing all of his highlights, creativity, finger rolls, and stats pop up, it was an inspiration for me to keep going. Don't get me wrong: there were a lot of guys who were playing in the NBA who had a frame like me, who may have shot a three-pointer or two (and that's all I used to do coming up), but there was nobody on that Hall of Fame level, nobody who had that level of sustained greatness over time. I felt different having a guy who I could directly relate to the way I did with George.

It was so inspirational, especially when I started winning scoring titles. When I won my first one, I thought about his first—the one he won against David Thompson when they went back and forth at the end of the season, and they scored 60 and 70 points in their final games battling for the title. That right there showed me what to strive for. Not that it was all about the scoring, but that was my impact on the game at that point. It's a standard that everybody holds once they become a great player, and our jobs are to set that standard every single night. Just knowing that those two were competing against each other and knowing how high they set that standard meant something to me.

* * *

When I first went up to Nike's campus in Portland, I was around 18 or 19 years old. One of the first things I saw was the ICEMAN poster with him sitting on the iced-out throne. That was the beginning of me seeing the other side of Ice—his brand, his persona, how people viewed him. Before then I was looking at him as just an athlete. Then I began to see the differences in how people in San Antonio and just people in the basketball community revered him. I started to say, "I want that, too." I wanted that respect.

It sunk in kind of early. It wasn't like I did a deep dive on him to learn his whole life top to bottom; it was just seeing little stuff sprinkled in of him here and there that kept me inspired. Not just as a ballplayer but as a person. And then once I got in the league, I had the opportunity to chop it up with him in my first couple of years, so everything came full circle. That was after a 2009 game in Oklahoma City. The NBA had set up a mentor program where some of the past greats were getting with some of the younger players in the league. At that time, Russell Westbrook, Jeff Green, and I were the young guys on the Thunder. And Ice was one of the guys who was there for us to get to know. We met at Mickey Mantle's Steakhouse, right there in Bricktown, after a game. We just went through *so* many stories. We talked about the game of basketball and how we both saw it. I was young and I had no idea what to even talk to Ice about. So I just sat back and listened. A lot. I don't really know how to really explain it, but it was just something special. At that age I didn't know exactly what I was doing, I was on a new team, new to the league, and I was sitting there talking to a legend, one that I'd been compared to for a large part of my basketball life. It just seemed so farfetched for me to even be sitting there talking to him. But as I got older, that moment sticks out more and more. It stayed with me 13, 14 years after the fact. It meant so much for me to meet Ice, especially at that point of my career. I tell people that story all of the time.

When I hear him say he sees himself in me, it just reassures me that the work I'm putting in is the right type of work. I learned that I like the accolades that come with playing in the NBA, the championships, the awards, and all of that, but getting the respect from the people who played in different eras, that's equal to a championship for me. Don't get me wrong: the rings, the championships, the All-Star appearances—all of that shit is incredible, but when I get that respect from the guys, who played through different decades of basketball, about my work ethic, production on the floor, and passion and love for the game, that means a lot. And for George, specifically, to spot that on me, well, I can tell he still has love for the game. So there's a sense of pride that comes with hearing it. It's sort of like I'm finishing some of the things that he and some of the greats weren't able to. It makes me want to keep pushing the game forward because they put me in position to do so.

I look at basketball through the lens of how groups of players in each era helped push the game to newer heights. He's simply part of that group who changed the game. Because of George, there was more scoring, more athleticism, more length at the guard position, more wiry frames—not just athletes with physical attributes—and more skills that started to come into the game during his time. George, along with 10-to-12 other guys, helped push the game to that next era, which feeds into guys like me who hopefully are going to feed the guys after us. And because of guys like Ice, we're always going to have someone we can go back and reference. Plus, Ice is so cool. His personality really is as cool as ice. He just sits back and does a lot, and nobody would ever know it. You don't hear about it. He's one of people I respect just for how he moves through life as a human being.

Personally, for me, just having him around is hard to put into words. We don't talk often, but he's one of the people I know I can talk to because he went through the same things that I've had to go through as a player. Add that to the ease in which he does things, the grace in which he gives what he gives to everybody, the caring, the heart that he has, he's someone who I can look at and say, *What would he do in this moment?* Ice has been one of those guys I sit back and ask myself if Ice would do it that way. He's someone I know will always be there without ever throwing himself on me. I've always had great respect and reverence for people like that.

Basketball is life. All of the lessons we learn as ballplayers bleed together and feed off one another. All of the lessons we get in life can be used both on and off the court. I'm just grateful in my life I've had the opportunity to be around somebody like Ice.

—Kevin Durant

EXORDIUM

Never been one of them kind of guys…

Because loyalty.

And then relationships. I think the biggest part of my life—and where I've have had a lot of my success—is relationships. With God, with my wife, with my children, with my teammates, I mean, I treat them how I want to be treated so I don't have many issues. All I have to do is look in the mirror to see how I want to be treated and I treat them that way. Very seldom does that lead to false hope.

My mom gave me that moral. At a very early age. She told me, "You treat people how you want to be treated." *Now am I perfect?* Nah, I'm not perfect, but I had a foundation to build off of. And what made me stay true to the foundation was that I believed in it. I had faith in it. Those are two strong words: *belief* and *faith*. Faith is a lot of times unseen until it's proven from knowledge from studying. That's how you get your faith. Like, I had faith in my jumper because I worked at it. Where else is it going to come from? My mind? People will lie to themselves and tell themselves things that aren't true because that's kinda the system we live in. But I've never been one of them kind of guys to boast about myself. I like putting in the work because I like seeing the results.

I believed in what I was doing and how I was pursuing it, knowing that it would make me better. For me, it's strictly fundamental. And I knew that no one could take that from me. It gave me a sense of ownership, a sense of satisfaction. And that comes with me *not* winning a championship. They critique and judge your career to the point that if you don't win a championship, you aren't successful! I don't buy into that narrative. Why should I? I know what it takes to win a championship. You gotta be healthy, you gotta have the right players, you gotta have the right coaches, everything gotta work. And I ain't never been one of those kinda guys that says, "Ah, man, I didn't have enough around me." Nope. I had enough around me to win it. We just didn't win it.

I've heard a lot of brothas say, "Man, you think if you had them kinda guys around you, you woulda won one?" I'm not caught up like that, never have been. And I knew we could win it in the '70s against the Washington Bullets when we were the last four teams. *I knew* we could win it; we just didn't. We were up 3–1! We just didn't do it. We had Artis Gilmore, Larry Kenon, James Silas, Billy Paultz. We could play and we had a great coach in Doug Moe, who gave me the green light and trusted me with it. Everybody doesn't get the green light. Because he trusted me, my teammates trusted me. And that ties into loyalty. Coach Moe would say: "George, what I need you to do is...shoot whenever you want to."

But that also meant I needed to get some of the other guys involved so that they wouldn't be thinking that it was just *my* team. I needed them to know that we could win because this was *our* team. Look I was The Man. There was no secret to that. But I didn't walk around like I was. And I didn't like anyone to tell me that. Don't tell me what I already know; tell me something else. But this game is designed to play one way: as a team.

I wasn't the kinda guy to win at all costs. I can say it like that. It didn't consume me like that. It consumes some guys. I don't think you should let anything consume you like that to where you lose and then go home and cry. One time I cried because we lost after being up 3–1 and we lost that game that would have put us in the NBA Finals. I was real mad because of that. But ain't nobody see me cry, and I cried because we let that opportunity slip away. We made negative history: losing after being up 3–1. So I was hurt in that aspect of the game. You don't get many chances to be there, to be in the semifinals, to be the last four teams.

The whole narrative of "But he ain't win" is scary. Pro athletes win. They win because they do things that very few did. Just because that person didn't win a championship shouldn't take away from things. In order to win a championship, certain aspects have to be in place. Everything has to fall into place. Michael Jordan didn't win for a long time before everything fell into place. But it still didn't take away from his greatness. What a lot of these dudes were doing for the game who didn't win championships was greatness to me. You can't let a superstar die in this league that still exists, whose legacy still exists. So if the people of today, who're running things, gonna let past superstars' stories and legacies die, then guys like me are gonna keep 'em alive.

It's not about me. It's never been about me. I already know I could play. Why I gotta tell you how good I am? You could come and see for yourself. I knew players had to be more than one-dimensional. So if you come at me one way, I'm coming at you another way. Now were there guys who made me work harder? No question! There were certain guys who made it easy; there were certain guys who didn't. I always say, "I got an easy 30 and I got a hard 30." Dennis Johnson made me get a hard 30, Michael Cooper made me get a hard 30, T.R. Dunn made me get a hard 30, Bobby Jones made me get a hard 30. But they weren't going to stop me from gettin' 30. And that's because it was really my own preparation. I had a lot of tools. I'd go to work and I'd go into my toolbox. If I needed a wrench, I'd get it; if I needed a screwdriver, I knew how to get one. I knew how to use both hands. I wasn't limited in what I could do with that basketball. Some players could make me use more tools than I necessarily wanted to use.

Hopefully, I played the game the right way. That's what I always tell myself. And I had some success—more individually than team-wise, and that's why I don't get celebrated the same as others. I might not have beat everyone, but I had 'em scared. And just because they won, doesn't mean they beat *me*. Guys today tell me stories all the time about myself that I marvel at because I can't believe that it's me who they are talking about. Before some game players would actually come up to me before the tip-off, stuttering, "Hey, Ice, Ice, don't, don't kill me tonight."

Once I heard that, I tried to get 50 points on 'em. I didn't have any mercy. Eddie Johnson, a hell of a shooter from Chicago, played for the Kansas City Kings as a rookie and said: "I was a rookie, and one game Ice was guarding me and I ran Ice through a pick, and Joe C. Meriweather hit with a hard one. *Boom.* And I got an open jump shot. On the next play down court, Gerv ran down next to me and said, 'Hey, hey young fella, lemme tell you this: you know—*you know*—I'm going to get mine, so next time just tell me when the pick's coming?'"

I know I was one of the greatest scorers of all time because of how I did it. I know it, and one day the masses are going to know it. And a perfect example of how it is slowly coming out is through the NBA2K games. It's not about personality; it's based on analytics. And now that they've included the analytics in the game, I'm one of the top players of the games because statisically I can't be denied. So now I'm up there with LeBron James analytically. When you look at analytics, that means production. One of the greatest honors I've received was the Seagrams 7 Award. I got that award for being the most efficient player in the league. And they did that analytically, by the numbers. Everything comes down to research.

I talk a lot, but I know you got to have humility. If you lose that, you lose you. Humility is what takes you to that next level. It means you care, it means you recognize. That's Godly. That's a trait the heavenly father gave us. Don't be all about yourself. Don't be boastful. Don't lose your ability to see, to grow, to stand back, and to appreciate others. That's why I would never say, "I'm the greatest scorer of all time." Even though sometimes I would think I was, I wouldn't say it. I'll let you be the one to make that choice. I'll let the stats do that.

It was a different era then in how the game was played. Back then I was getting 40 on you, and you could hold, grab, push me. You get 40 now, and no one can touch you. I was 185 pounds and being defended by guys who were 215, 230. They put their hands on me back when that was legal, and I still got 40. The game's evolved. I ain't mad at it. Guys make beaucoup money—and I'm a part of that foundation—but how you spend it is on you. We were a part of helping people have an opportunity to make it. I hate that the NBA Players Association doesn't keep us close to these young guys to help educate them. I always wished that we had a program where we would get together with these young players and just talk because it's not about how much you make. It's about how you learn how to keep, how you learn how to treat what you make. We already know guys who've lost $100 or 200 million. I'm sad for them. We've got to teach them how to build wealth, man. And that takes wisdom. I always tell the young cats, "Y'all ain't got nothin' but a wealthy man writing rich men checks."

You need to hang around some folks who've been around wealth, who've come up the same way you have and listen to them. I'm not even going to call it advice. Just talk to them. Sit down and talk to a brotha like me, someone that's going to care about you all. I don't want nothing from them. All I want to do is give them the wisdom I got. I'm 70 years old, I'm with that same woman I started out with, got three lovely babies and seven grandkids, and in the end, that's what's going to matter. All this other stuff everyone else is talking about will go away, and I don't want them to continue to get caught up in that. I think that's how we lose our babies, that's where we lose these young players. They get too caught up and want to be the king. Who you gonna rule? Be the king of your own castle. Rule that.

It's a hard journey we're on. The NBA has a lot of turns and twists, downfalls, and success. But in the end: where are you at in your life? Do you still have your sanity? Do you still have your self-worth? Can you help somebody else? It's our jobs to tell people, to help people. But in the end, it's up to them. I heard the Ball dad, LaVar, say something about his son LaMelo talking to Jordan when they drafted him. He was asked, "You think LaMelo's gonna talk to Mike?"

"What the hell he gonna talk to Mike for?" he said. *"Mike ain't played in 27 years!"* I started laughing. You need to talk to someone who has the kind of success that Jordan has especially when it comes down to money. That brotha there has put himself in a place where I don't think anyone else who's played the game—any game really—has ever been. I got nothing but respect for Jordan. It would be really a good one for these young players to be able to talk with Jordan if they can. It's a privilege. Talk about something more than just basketball. Because another LaMelo can come just as quick as the first one in this game, buddy. We get so caught up in seeing "the next" somebody that we forget we saw someone who was pretty good, too. Over the years I've heard, "Man, I never seen no one like that!" People never thought they'd see another Ice.

It's the game, man. It's our livelihood. It's no different than the gladiators. Same circumstance. We're getting paid to entertain for people; that's our job. But it can't be your life. If players keep that perspective that this game is my job and this is not my life, I think we'll have a lot more kids in the game doing a lot more things to help others, to help somebody else. We have a responsibility, man, to help these youngsters be better young men. I'm a relationship guy. I look at this game and my life in those terms. I'm not looking at it in terms of me being great. Instead, I'm looking at the relationships I've been able to have with these people from around the world just for playing this game.

CHAPTER ONE

NBA 75

There's only one way to get into that room.

There are a lot of guys who've played this game a long time, and to be included as one of the 75 best to ever do it is an honor that I wasn't ever looking for. When we were all together before halftime of the All-Star Game in Cleveland, you could feel it. There was an aura. I never considered myself when I was playing. I always wanted to be good and I put the work in to prepare myself to be the best that I could, but I never did it for the purpose to be a Hall of Famer, top 50, or top 75. So to be honored as one is a great honor. It's like you do something, you work hard, you do your best, and in the end, somebody rewards you for your work. It's an unbelievable honor. I wasn't expecting it.

I played against some greats and I watched some—the guys before me, the Jerry Wests and Oscar Robertsons, the Dave Bings—and all I wanted was to be able to have that chance to do what they were doing. Now, everyone plays for a different reason. But when I was looking around that room, I was seeing players like Bing and I'm like, *Wow, I'm in the same room that brotha's in*. I remember how I looked up to him because he was in Detroit, playing for the Pistons. He once coached me in a high school All-Star Game where I got MVP, and Bing told me, "Man you keep playing like this you're gonna be playing against me." Which I did. So for me to see that, hear things like that, and to be in the same room and be recognized for the same reason, it's just…humbling.

It's special to tell them how much I appreciate them and how much they inspired me. You get that more in my era and in the older players' eras than in this era. I know us in the '80s and '90s inspired a lot of guys playing today. They are just not as vocal about it today as we were yesterday.

West told me, "Man, you are one of the guys I'd pay to see play." I heard West say that—and we all know who West was, and this is after his career—in the locker room in L.A. at The Forum. Man, I'm 70 now and I never forget that yet. Same with what Bing told me. And I was 16, 17 years old when he told me that. I still remember it, I still hold on to it. Words like that are a gift.

Let another brotha know how you feel, what you did for them. It's important. It's important to carry it on. We're in a brotherhood and ain't too many of us in it. There are other guys watching us, and we need to make sure we pass it down. You motivate to teach, and I felt there was a lot of education in that room, a lot of love and respect in that room for guys who played before you. For everyone in there, there were guys in there who played before them. And what some of the new guys don't fully realize is that they all gonna be an "ex" someday. And it's going to be quicker than you think. I laugh about that, but all in all, it was beautiful to be in that room of 75. Kevin Durant wasn't there, but James Harden was. At one point Harden was standing next to me, and the photographers told him to move to the left. Everyone busted out laughing, saying "Him? Going to the left?" I told him: "Yeah, James, you go left, but you still put up 50 on 'em." He averaged 36.1 points in 2018–19. It's unbelievable to be able to put up those kind of numbers for a year. I topped out at 33. You gotta be ballin', you gotta be athletic, skillful, and smart to get big numbers like that. So it was good to see him in the room.

I grew up with Robertson because he and my high school coach, Willie Merriweather, went to Crispus Attucks High together in Indianapolis, and Merriweather became a teacher in Detroit and became my high school coach. It was good seeing Robertson. And, of course, Bing. You realize there's only one way there, there's only one way to get into that room: work hard, build up your confidence because you can do the things that you are trying to do on the floor. And we got all kind of ways to motivate each other, and I know a lot of the guys still playing, who were in that room, were motivated to see the history of the game that they'd be able to stand next to and be recognized as one of the greats.

Obviously, we all have our thoughts on who could've made it, but then you'd be taking someone else off. That's why I don't do that. I played against a bunch of great ones who I know were great because they played against me. Every time we saw them, they got 40 points on us. It's an unfortunate situation not being recognized, but in life that sometimes is how things work out. Whenever you put a hard number on something, someone is going to get left out. Also, you gotta take into consideration the ones who were voting. I know it had to be hard. They had to sit up there and look at thousands of guys' careers. Whether you agree with it or not, these are the ones who are going to be celebrated. And in the end, I'm appreciative that I'm one of those 75. Even if I am No. 75.

And if you're on the NBA 50, which was also celebrated in Cleveland during the All-Star Game in 1997, it's hard not to make the NBA 75! Even with the revoting, no one got taken off, and that was a good thing. I saw the narrative the NBA was using. You had some young guys who'd only been in the league a few years, but all of them are legit. That's what I appreciate about it. Being a San Antonio Spur, I'm a Kawhi Leonard fan. So it was good to see him on there. KD, he's probably my favorite. Glad he's on there. And Steph Curry. I gotta chance to holla at him while we were all there, but we didn't talk about ball. He and I are big-time golfers, so we talked golf. He also mentioned his dad to me. That meant a lot to me. I love the relationship that they have. I love to see that bond between the two of them. I'm a dad. So I know how special that bond is. But I said to Curry: "Heard, you been hitting your ball, man." And he just lit up! But what I didn't get to tell him was about his wife. I have her cookbooks that I use all of the time. And I meant to tell him, "Can you tell your wife I *love* her recipes?" And I saw Giannis Antetokounmpo. I shook his hand. He belongs.

I am proud to be a part of that group of 75. I celebrated with them, I celebrated for them. The whole weekend was good, but for that one day in the arena before they introduced us to walk on that court, I mean, you are in a room full of greatness. It was beautiful. That's the only word you can use. What's so beautiful to me is that it wasn't 1–75; it was we are all *the* 75. We. That's powerful. Now people can write whatever kind of scenario they want saying who's No. 1, who's No. 2, and so on, but I don't look at it like that. No one in that room looked at it like that. Not on that day. When I was in that room, I looked at it as these are the top 75 of all time. Now you can put Kareem Abdul-Jabbar No. 1, Michael Jordan No. 2, Wilt Chamberlain No. 3, Bill Russell No. 4, but no, it don't work like that. All of those networks can try to spin it however they want, but in my heart, I believe every player in that room was thinking: *I'm among the top 75 guys who played the game in the history of the NBA.* And I was in the room looking at them, and they were looking at me. *Beautiful* is the perfect word to describe it.

We all just started to mingle with one another. Once you get a bunch of men together, you know we all got jokes, we all got personalities. Here comes Dennis Rodman! He's definitely one, DRod. I gotta chance to coach him and some of the things he was doing in the game; he definitely was a part of that honor. We 75 are all different. We brought our own different greatness to the game. Just seeing everyone with the smiles on their faces when we were standing up on that stage to take that picture, everyone appreciating where they were at, what they'd all done, it just brought me back to remembering that the game was designed to be played one way, and that's as a team. Even though we were all individuals up there, in order to be there you had to be great inside of the game's concept of team. All teams ain't gonna win it all, but to be able to shine within a team atmosphere and be named one of the 75 best players of all time, c'mon, man, that's hard to beat.

Now if asked if I'd rather be a part of this group or have won an NBA championship, I'd rather be part of this group. I understand that only one team can win a championship a year, and things gotta be right in order to win it, but to be honored like this you had to be consistent. You had to be in love with it for a long time, for most—if not all—of your life. For me it wasn't all of my life; it was a part of my life that I gave my life to. I put my soul into it. So I knew what it took to be the best that I could be playing the game. I don't think people look at it like that. They try to look at it like, *Well, he didn't win a championship man. So, man, he shouldn't be illuminated when we start taking about greatness.*

And I'm like, *Fo' real? Hard as I worked to try to get a championship? And you know—just like I do—how hard it is to win one?* And a lot of guys didn't start winning until the team put that supporting cast around them to win, to make them even shine more. And I'm not saying I didn't have it. I'm just saying I didn't win it. I had a championship team around me. We just didn't win it. I would never say I didn't have a supporting cast. I had a chance to win it all. It just didn't happen. There are a whole lot of guys who played that game who won championships that ain't a part of this group here. This is a special group. They mess with Charles Barkley about that all of the time, mostly because he's on TV. Shaquille O'Neal and the TNT guys tease him. Karl Malone, John Stockton, Patrick Ewing, Elgin Baylor, me, and the guys in the 75 who don't have rings just didn't win a championship.

I'm a God-fearing man. If you've been studying a long time about the truth about God and I start studying and learn the same thing that you do, we'll all get the same reward. If I start late but come away with the same knowledge as you, we're gonna get the same reward, and that's everlasting life. That's me in the spiritual way, but it applies to how we are. I looked at my bag with the jacket in it, saying to myself, *There's only 75 of them. In. Basketball. History.* When you see someone carrying that bag or wearing that jacket, he's one of the 75. That's how you distinguish yourself when you are part of a group that's 75 strong. It makes no difference who got there first, how long they been in, how many championships, All-Star Games, scoring titles you won. It's all your works recognized, and no one is greater than the other. The day after, I got on the plane and I saw someone's 75 bag and I was trying to figure out who's bag it was. Turns out, it was Elgin's wife. I thought, *Oh yeah, she part of the 75.*

I'll probably never wear the jacket. It's symbolic. I'm not that vain to be walking around with an honor, a trophy of sorts. Now some people are, and I ain't mad at them. Paul Pierce had his on during the NBA Finals, supporting the Boston Celtics while they were playing the Golden State Warriors. And I get that for him. One thing I've always said: you can pull up in a Rolls and get out, and people will be looking at you, but I can pull up in a Volkswagen and get out, and they'll be saying, "Here comes Ice."

* * *

It's more than ball for me. I thought about that over that weekend. How I got in that room came from my high school coach. He showed interest in me as a young man, and that's what I needed at that time. Coach Merriweather gave me that opportunity to have confidence in myself. And that's when I grew six inches to 6'6", and then the head coach wanted me.

I was able to maintain staying in love with this game because to me it was a skill, one that I was able to hone in on. It took a lot of hard work. I endured a lot of pain to get and stay in shape. You love it, then you fall in love with it over the course of time because you became pretty good at it. It did a lot for me. It gave me a lot of exposure as a human being, took me around the world, helped me raise a family and be able to take care of them. I'm a part of the foundation of this game to be what it's become today. And without a solid foundation, the game can't grow. And without that foundation, the game might not be what it is today. How is that not going to make you feel honored, humbled, special to know that you were a part of something that grew to be global? When we started out, we weren't global. When I was playing, there were about four or five Europeans in the league. Now there are a great number of Europeans playing in the NBA. My franchise in San Antonio won championships with European players, and I'm a part of that! A lot of them watched me play. After I was retired, the Spurs were playing in France and they introduced me and they made me cry in a sense because they gave me an ovation. I'm like, *We're in France. How they know about me?* And that's what kept me loving the game. I see that I was a part of this game's fabric.

As I got older, I saw how the game could better my life and my family's life and get us out of the circumstances we grew up in and how it ended up working out that way, but as a kid, I never looked at it that way. I never looked at it like I gotta play ball cause I gotta get out of these streets, I gotta get outta the hood. I never looked at what the game could do for me. I was in love with the game, I just loved playing it. I never had that mind-set of even being a pro. I never thought about that. I started late. I really started getting interest in the game around 13 or 14 years old. My brothers played, and I always just wanted to beat them. I can honestly say that I never looked at basketball as something that was going to save me. Coming up, being raised by a single mom, education was what she always put on us. That's how she said we were going to get out and have opportunities. She always said, "Education will create opportunities for you."

We were poor, but she did such an unbelievable job that we never felt like we were poor. I never knew what rich was, I didn't know what well off was, but I knew I wasn't hungry. I knew I didn't have the same clothes as some of the guys had, but I wasn't insecure. And I was a dull, little kid coming up. I was. And I didn't have many expectations. But that's what makes the start of my basketball journey amazing because I really got a chance to be a kid. You know what I mean? I really got a chance to grow up, have fun, waiting on the ice cream truck, tamale man, all of that stuff. All the kid stuff. I grew up when I was supposed to, the way I was supposed to. And that's because of my mother. She dedicated her life to us.

Once I made the high school team, I started kinda looking at the game as more than just fun and into a responsibility thing. I didn't play junior high or elementary, I literally just played in high school. As a freshman I was trying to play, I was trying to make the team. I was too little. I was 5'9" as a freshman. When I became a sophomore, thangs changed. I could play. People started noticing me. I still had no expectations of really going to college and all that. I was just playing the game. In the moment, nothing more.

I never looked ahead and definitely didn't look back. I didn't know how good I was when it came to basketball, I mean they kept saying I was good, but to me I was just hoopin'. Then I grew. Then I got to my senior year, I started hanging out with my hero, Ralph Simpson, and started going out to Lansing, Michigan. Then, I started getting pretty good by then. Charles Tucker was up there, and I got to know him and started spending time with him and them guys in Lansing. That's when I realized I was just as good as most. I was averaging 31 points and 20 rebounds. We went to the city championship and lost. Then we went to the state and lost. Once I got into it, I never let anything get in the way. Like the sun didn't shine if I didn't work out, if I didn't hoop.

It's the difference between love and being in love. I was in love with the game. So it never was a burden, I never felt like playing was a burden, something I had to do. It was just as much a part of me as putting on my clothes every day. I was like a horse with a bridle and blinkers on; I was just looking in one direction to get better. It was easy. I never minded shooting 500 jumpers a day. I ain't mind playing anyone one-on-one. And I played a lot of one-on-one in the early part because that's what was available. When you practice a lot, ain't a lot of people doing the same thing. I didn't know how valuable that was going to be, but I played a lot of one-on-one. I tell people today—even once I got into the pros—I played a lot of one-on-one with certain guys who were on teams I was on. Big guys, little guys. It didn't do anything but make me better. That's where I found out I could score. *On anybody.* And that came from the work, and that's what I've always taken a certain amount of pride in because I was good at that. I was good at preparation. And that to me is how I ended up in that room.

CHAPTER TWO

ANGEL

It was almost like an angel took care of me.

My mom died four years ago. She was 90. With my understanding about resurrection, I knew that she was just going to sleep. And I wanted her to. I handled her death more spiritually than anything. She was suffering in the end. Her last two, three weeks of her life, she was going through a lot of pain. Her quality of life was gone. She was like a vegetable. Obviously, it hurts not to see her here anymore, but in reality she really wasn't there. Her body was, but *she* wasn't. Some of my brothers and sisters took it harder than others, but I have hope that I'll see her again. So it's encouraging me to keep doing the right things so that I will.

She had a full life. Boy, she worked. She worked for us. We didn't feel poor, but we were. I'm from a food stamp family. I'd go to the store with my friends, and they had money and I had food stamps and I'd try to wait until they got done buying their food so they wouldn't see my food stamps. I stood in bread lines, wore goodwill clothes, had Detroit Goodfellows boxes, all the government stuff: cheese, crackers, soup. To this day, when I don't have anything else to lean on, I lean on those memories of the things she used to have us do. We had coal stoves, so when it was my turn, I had to go out in that 10-degree cold and find wood to start the fire to get the house warm for the rest of the family. Unbelievable memories. Sometimes those bread lines would be so long. We'd wait 30 to 40 minutes to get that one bag of bread that would sometimes be moldy, but you had to take it. We'd cut around that mold and eat that bread. I definitely was not raised with a silver spoon—or a spoon at all. I was the best peanut butter and jelly maker in the world. My brothers and sisters would come to me, "George, come spread my peanut butter across my bread." I had the touch back then.

Detroit was all we knew. East side. On the corner of Field Street and Saint Paul. I tell my kids, "We were raised in the hood; y'all are suburb kids." Totally different survival atmosphere than what I came up in. My mom told me a long time ago: "George, treat people like you want to be treated, and you ain't gonna have very many problems in life." That meant a lot to me. It still does, and I still live by it.

As I got older, I realized how much Mom loved me. Mom didn't tell me she loved me a lot. She showed it. She showed me how dedicated she was to us as her children. I was raised by a mom who had to work all of the time while raising six kids: Barbara, Booker, Claude, Francis, Derrick, and me. She had to work so hard to take care of us. I really only totally learned that when I got older and started having a family of my own. Then I started to really understand the sacrifice she made with her life. My mom used to love to dance, but as we got older, I never saw her dance. She lost a lot of the things that she loved to do because she had children and she had to raise them by herself. I guess in the end what that told me was how much she loved us and what it takes to maintain your own family. When you start talking about the most important things in life, Mom was my hero.

My two older brothers, Booker and Claude, were big influences on me coming up. I just watched them. Both of them played ball. Both of them worked at it. They were both into building their bodies up, doing calisthenics with weights, push-ups, sit-ups, pull-ups, and all of that kinda stuff. And Booker was pretty dominant in high school in the city of Detroit. And we were stair-step kids, one right underneath the other. And once one left, I began to face my own challenges in life. My oldest brother moved on, so I didn't get a chance to spend that much time with him, and my other brother kinda fell off. So we didn't get to spend that much time together. And then I became a pro at 19, so I was gone. And then my younger brother, Derrick, who's 11 years younger and who also played for the New Jersey Nets a couple of years, was under me, and I didn't get enough time to spend with him because I was gone, and my life had started. We spent childhood together, but we didn't spend that young adulthood together. And that's the most important part; that's when the influences really come in. You almost grow apart. You start having your own friendships, and they almost become closer than your brothers. Once you go off into the world, you become really close with other people because you spend so much time with them.

And there are a lot of Gervins I don't know. My dad and mom divorced, so there are more Gervins. I had a dad that I didn't ever really know, though I know he had a mental health issue because he was an alcoholic. And my dad had another family; I have some step-brothers and step-sisters that I don't even know. I've gone my whole life not knowing some of them. Yeah, we got the same last name, we're family-tied, but we don't know each other. And it's not like I don't want to know them, but at this stage of our lives, we hardly have time for ourselves. We're raising our own families. But that becomes another obstacle you gotta deal with and one we have to understand. But I know my step-family exists because I told my mom not to go down there and be nosy, but she did.

Black women coming up in the '40s and '50s went through some trauma. The laws weren't the same. They'd get married, the man would leave you, and leave you with all those kids. That's what happened to my mom. We were in Detroit; his other family was in Georgia. That was hard on her. That hurt her. She went down there and found out about his family and came back miserable. I used to always ask other kids, guys I played ball with when I was coming up: "You gotta mom and a dad?" When they'd say yes, I'd always say, "Wow, you lucky."

But once I grew up, I was glad they weren't together. Just to have a dad? Not if they were killing each other inside. I learned about the long history he had: the police record, the beatings he used to give her. She never let me see the ugly part. She never told me any of that, but my sisters told me. She never told me because she was trying to protect me. That's a true mom.

* * *

I was real little when I was coming up. I was only 5'9" as a freshman at Martin Luther King Jr. High School. The year I got there, the school moved from East Grand Boulevard to East Lafayette Boulevard and changed its name from Eastern High School to Martin Luther King Jr. High School not long after he was assassinated.

Coach Merriweather saw something in me. He saw the skills and stuck with me. The way Coach Krzyzewski's players feel about him, that's how I feel about Merriweather. You saw how many of Coach K's former players came out to see his last home game at Duke. There were like 90 of them. How big is that? I said before the game, "Oh, he gonna cry." And it's for a good reason. He was going to realize how many lives he's touched, and that's like me with Merriweather. He was with me since high school when I was a reserve on the bench. He's the one who kept me on the team. I might not even have a career if he didn't have that belief in me. The head coach said, "Naw, he can't play."

And it was Merriweather who said to the head coach, "Let me put him on the reserves. He's got moves and stuff." Even though the head coach really didn't believe in me, Merriweather took an interest, for whatever reason. That's why this game is more than ball for me. So the next year, I grew and brought the skills with me. Then I could finish. Both hands. Left. Right. Merriweather taught me to understand the importance of balance. He worked with my back to the basket. He really helped build up my foundation, my fundamentals. Taught me how important they were, and I got sound. Once you have that, you can add stuff, and that's what I was able to do. He took me to the next level. And that was when my career really began.

And off the court he was almost like a second father. And then there was Dr. Robert Sims, a Public School League doctor in Detroit. He was the other one who had a big influence on my life. He taught me the little things. Every boy needs a man in their life, and these guys were the men in my life. They knew I didn't know my dad. He wasn't in our lives at all, and Mom could only do so much with boys because once you grow up into becoming a young man, grown men become important. And those were the two men I feel had the most influence on me in a positive way. Both of them were successful. Merriweather was in education, and Dr. Sims, who also worked for General Motors for 40 to 50 years, had his own medical practice. He's in his 90s now and lives in Houston. One of my golf buddies, Sims still hits the links with me. Both of them, Sims and Merriweather, gave me guidance and confidence.

Merriweather came up in the '40s. He played ball with Oscar Robertson in high school in Indiana. So obviously they went through some tough times with social justice because you know Indiana during those days was not the best place for us. Birthplace of the Klan. Merriweather could have played pro ball. He was that good. But the military called, and that stopped him. Then during his time in the military, he realized how important education was. So he went to school, went to Purdue, and then he came to Michigan and became a teacher. Everybody knew him in the city of Detroit. He may have taught 10,000 kids over the 44 years he was an educator. If he ended up being a ballplayer, I don't know what direction I would have gone.

I mean, I had other interests as a young man. I was big into electronics, which was probably my favorite subject in school. But honestly I really don't know what would have happened in my life had Merriweather not been a part of it. It coulda been a flip. I coulda lost interest in the game. As a kid it was a pivotal time. We were God-fearing people, but being from the inner city, you never know. It was almost like an angel took care of me because if I don't have that interest it's real easy to get lost in another interest. So that angel put me in a system where I could grow, and that was in sports. And basketball was the only sport I liked. I didn't like any other sport once I set my sights on playing basketball. By the time I was a senior, I was averaging 31 points and 20 rebounds a game for MLK.

We all are not born in the same type of circumstances. I was raised without a father, without any type of relationship with my father, but Merriweather and Dr. Sims were the men in my life. A lot of our babies—and by that I meant kids—don't get hugged a lot. They didn't have many people to just pull them to the side and put their arms around them and say, "Come here, man, you know I care about you."

Merriweather didn't give out a lot of hugs, but he gave me hugs in his own way. They weren't natural hugs, where you can feel the warmth of someone when they put their arms around you, but he'd take me out to eat, get them Big Boy hamburgers. Big Boy was big back in them days, in the '60s and '70s. Those were the type of hugs that he gave me. Not a literal hug, but it meant just as much. I still felt that warmth. He'd take me over to his house. I knew each of the three women he would marry. I literally became a part of his life. He never gave up and he gave me a chance.

I remember one class besides Merriweather's class I had in high school. It was Mr. Whipper's biology class. He also took an interest in me. He used to take his time with me, taught me how to wash my hands correctly, wash my finger nails, all that stuff. He showed an interest in me that made me want to do good for him in his class. And I ended up getting a B out of his class. His and Merriweather's classes are the only two I really remember from high school. And that bothered me. Still does.

To this day, I still don't know why I didn't listen to my mom when it came to education. She'd tell me a lot, but it was on me to put in the work at school. It's a mystery to me how I got out of school. I go to bible study with Merriweather now and I don't bring it up because I don't want it to be a reflection on him, but I still don't know. I'm still baffled today about my education. Back then we got graded A, B, C, D, or E. There were no Fs, and I had all Es. My mom tore me up. All Es really meant no effort. My sister used to do me like this: "How'd George get the same grade I got?" I'd say, "Because I copied off your paper."

I didn't have any interest when it came to school. So technically I failed. I had to sit out a half a year. Then I got it back together the following year. But still I got a blank envelope instead of a diploma. I didn't even look inside of it because I knew wasn't nothing in there. I had to go to night school and day school at the same time in order to just get a certain grade point average so that I could go to college. Grade-wise that's what kept me from having a better opportunity to play for big colleges because basketball-wise I qualified. I was All-State in the state of Michigan. So grades were the only reason the bigger schools and the schools in the area weren't recruiting me. My grades were that bad. I tell young guys: "If you get good grades, you can go where you want to go. If you get bad grades, you gotta go where somebody else wants you to go."

That's the separation. So there were two sides to it back then, but now you don't have to go to college. But for us, if you had good grades, you could go anywhere, and everybody wanted you. Bad grades put your future in someone else's hands, and you probably ended up at a place where you didn't really want to go.

While I had to go to night school, I didn't really go that often. But basketball was my destiny. George Trapp, who was from Detroit, was playing at Long Beach State University in California and he told their coach at the time, Jerry Tarkanian, about me, and Tark came up to see me hoop in some recreational and the old AAU games and at St. Cecilia's. And after watching me, Tark just said, "I'll take him."

I was right out of high school, and back then you couldn't play as a freshman. You had to wait until your sophomore year to have eligibility to play in the NCAA. But to Tark I must have been worth the wait. I really didn't get to know Tark, didn't get to spend that much time with him because the coaches really couldn't be around the players who were freshmen that much. So all I did was really stay in the gym. But I was only there for a couple of weeks. It was 2,000 miles away from home, and that Santa Ana wind was blowing everywhere. I called my mom and said, "I don't know what's going on with all of this wind and stuff, but I don't like it here. I wanna come home."

Plus, I just didn't like being away from home so I came back. I got on a red-eye flight. I had money so I bought my own plane ticket, and the guy, whose place I was taking on the team, that brotha found me a car and got me a ride to the airport. He was so happy to see me go that he said, "I'll take you to the airport." And I never spoke to Tark. I just left. I left at midnight and got to Detroit early in the morning, and Dr. Sims picked me up. Then a few days later, Tark came back to Detroit to get me. He showed up to the Franklin Sullivan, a training center in my neighborhood in East Detroit, because he knew I was always there on Saturdays. He came in the gym, walking all slow like Tark does. We talked. And I told him, "Coach, this don't have anything to do with you, man. I miss home, miss my girl, miss my mom, and stuff. I ain't never been nowhere. C'mon, you know that. I'm from the eastside of Detroit. You took me way out to LaLa land, California, next to an ocean? Look: I'd love to play for you. But I'm not ready. I wanna come home."

At the time all Tark wanted to do was beat UCLA. He had Trapp on his squad. He also had Ed Ratleff who was playing guard at 6'6", and they would've had me. Tark said, "We can beat UCLA next year if we had Gervin." And we probably would have if I'd stayed. In his book he said, "What would I have been if I'd had George Gervin?"

I almost wanted to tell him, "Tark, let it go. Let it go, buddy. I love you, too."

Tark was that guy who always took the wayward kid and turned him around. He always took the kid who other people and places would question. He'd take guys, who just didn't do well in their younger years in school, and reshape them. Tark was good with us, good for us. And I say "us," even though I never played for him because I was still one of those kids back then who he gave an opportunity to. And all the guys, who ever played for him, loved him.

Then Jim Dutcher, who was the coach at Eastern Michigan University, came to my home and got me. So I was just in the right place at the exact right time with the exact right situation for me. I found the right coach to let me go on and showcase my talents. Then after an incident, which I'll get into later, I withdrew from Eastern Michigan and I just happened to be at the right place. When I got home, the owner of the Continental Basketball League, Roy White, gave me a chance to play in Pontiac, Michigan, 30 miles away from Detroit. Then Johnny "Red" Kerr saw me in the CBL. I was in the right situation, and he knew the right guy—Earl Foreman from the Virginia Squires in the ABA—and told Foreman to give me a shot. So that whole early part of my life and how I got through it all by being in those right places all of those times is amazing to me.

As much as my mom talked about education, it's like I went to sleep on it. I had to have because everybody from my family graduated from high school. My brothers, my sisters had scholarships to college. I mean, they got it done. But high school for me was just…different.

What was I doing? I'm asking myself even now. It's scary, especially when I think about other guys who were just as talented as me because Detroit brings out a lot of talent. I think of Clifford Pratt; he was a pro to me. Larry Fogle was a pro to me, and so was Lindsay Harrison. Coniel Norman got in, Eric Money got in, but ain't that many guys who I played against who made it to the league despite having the talent. It makes me wonder, *Why me?*

The only answer I can come up with is spiritual. That's the only thing I can think of. Jehovah draws you. That's the only way you're going to get to know God. Guys who had promising futures as high school basketball players, I see them, hug them, remind them of the challenges we had and the competition we had. And for some of them, life was rough. But *why me?* I feel everyone deserves an opportunity, but at the same time, I know life ain't like that. Choices we make and circumstances determine a lot. I made it from the bottom to the top and can't understand why. I'm humbled by it. I was on the floor with a lot of those guys, and a lot of those guys were just as good as I was. All of us had the potential to take it to the next level. What is the only thing that can separate you from men? That's God. He's the one who protects you. My favorite saying: everybody needs a somebody. And I wonder where these guys' somebodys were at? That's what bothers me more than anything else because they were just as good as I was. I had some unbelievable battles against them guys. I lost some of them battles against them and now I'm losing them in life. Before they died they had so many other issues. Mental health issues. Drugs and alcohol, which are still connected to mental health.

I just look at my journey. My wife says that I almost downplay my career and how successful I was, but I don't talk about education a lot and I say to her, "Honey, my journey when it comes to my education is dark." I can't see my high school years, I can't see the educational part. The learning, the classrooms, the desks, the teachers. When I was in middle school, I used to sign my name on pieces of paper *during the whole class*. All I'd do is write, "George Gervin, George Gervin, George Gervin" over and over. One of my best friends had one of those pieces of papers up until about 10 years ago. But those are the only things I remember. So that became a mental health issue for me as I got older. I always felt insecure when it came to spelling, math, geometry, the things that you learn in school. And when I got around people who were educated, I always felt a little insecure. I felt ashamed at times because I didn't think I knew anything in those circles. We all know how important grades one through 12 are when it comes to education for what you are about to experience in life. You have to have some of those fundamentals in order to be thought of as being successful. As I grew up, I started being around people who were educated. So I started questioning myself.

As I got older, I always talked in a way that I call "elementary." People understand what I am saying, but I only say words that I know. I do a lot of public speaking. I call them "talks" because people stand up and give me an ovation versus a speaker who people will just clap for. If I talk to you, you're more likely to really listen. But it was still a struggle of mine to deal with that. The fact that people understood me made me realize that I was a lot more educated than

I thought. I found out that I was pretty bright. I learned through my journey, not in the typical way. But I'm still not fully comfortable with it, and it all goes back to my education.

What I think about is how my mom always stressed education to us and how it didn't catch on with me. My mom used to whoop me, and I loved her for it because I used to get a whoppin' all the time when she got my grades. She used to say, "I ain't gonna let you just get away with anything! There's rules, there's laws, there's discipline. And when I tell you something, you gotta get it done."

I love that. I needed that. I'm glad my mom pulled off that ironing cord off the old iron and used it. That became my education. Little did she know the values, morals, and principles that she instilled in me was the education that I needed to handle the world that I was involved in and the one I was getting ready to face. The School of Life. You never graduate from it, but you learn to deal with. That's what she prepared me for. Now, my mom and I might have both been a little disappointed in where I was headed educationally in my primary years, but she was setting me up, and neither one of us knew it. She became my educator. If I hadn't had that value system that she gave me, I might not have been able to overcome the tribulations that came at me. She always talked about education and the power of it, but she gave me the formula to deal with life.

CHAPTER THREE

FRIENDS AND FOUNDATION

I had no understanding of the foundation I was laying down.

Throughout my whole career, I never worried about what somebody else made. I never got caught up in that. Yes, you try to get in life what you feel you deserve, but you have to be content with your situation. In this system we live in, so many people don't have anything. Be content with the things that you have because there are so many who don't have nothin'. C'mon, that's biblical. And what you get is enough to take care of you for where you are at in the world. My outlook on life all stems from that value system my mom placed in me. Treat people how you want to be treated is a real foundation on how I tried to live. And if you believe and live by that set of values, then you don't worry about what somebody else got. I was always satisfied with the things I had. I never had that greed grow inside of me, never became a boastful person, bragging about myself. Certain traits breed ugly stuff in us.

One of the top football players out of our area was Sam Mansell. Back in the day in the 1960s, we were going through a lot with the riots, the unrest, the disturbances in the schools. We used to have to have meetings in school auditoriums throughout Detroit, and Mansell was one of the leaders athletic-wise as well as being one of the spokespersons of the city. One day we were in the school cafeteria at Martin Luther King Jr. High, and he made a statement: "That's one thing I like about George Gervin. He's one of the baddest guys to play this game, but he don't never run around talking about he this or that he's that."

There was a guy from high school, Jesse King. We were two bad brothas. He was my teammate. The two of us together, we were deadly, ain't no question. He could play, and I was pretty good during that time. I tried to get him in the pros for a long time, but it just didn't work out. He was about 6'6", and I thought he was just as good as I was in high school, and he had a good college career. But then there were circumstances. I brought him down to the Virginia Squires, got him into their camp. I brought him down to the San Antonio Spurs, got him into camp. I thought he played well enough, but he just didn't make it. It just didn't work out. He ended up not liking me later on in life, and it really hurt me. I didn't do anything to him, but my circumstance may have made him not like me as we got older. And once someone don't like you and you haven't done anything to them, that becomes their own issue, which is really a sickness, too. And now he's gone, no longer here. His brother used to tell me all of the time, "I don't know what's wrong with my brother, G, but you ain't did nothing to him."

That was a relief for me to hear him say that because I didn't. I tried to get him in the league. But life sometimes just brings so much at us at times, and over the years, he and I just didn't ever hook back up. Not like I thought we could have. And that impacted me, hurt me. Things happen to us in our lives that we just can't digest. You can't regurgitate it, you can't get rid of it. It sticks with you and then it becomes a sickness, one that ends up destroying you inside.

I also grew up with a guy named Leslie Martin. We were real tight, close in high school. He was a football player, definitely could have been a pro, and some of the people he knew felt that if I made it, I should've taken care of him. He didn't feel that way, but his people did because we were that close. When I went to Long Beach after graduation, he went to Long Beach, too. I kinda told the school, "Well, y'all can bring him in on a football scholarship." So they brought him in. But it just didn't work out. When I became a pro and I came out to San Antonio, I brought him with me until I brought my wife with me. With him, my wife—my girlfriend at the time—and I in the house, you know that's not going to last. She ain't mine *and* his girl. So I had to make a choice. But he was probably one of the closest guys to me in the early part of my pro career. Another longtime friend is James Morgan, who I call "Bull." Bull and I have done a lot together. He and I went to elementary, middle school, high school, and college together. And Bull's still with me. He never put any of that "man, you gotta make it for us" pressure on me.

I used to love taking things like lights apart and fixing them like electronics. I had other things that I enjoyed besides ball because I didn't play ball to be a pro. I didn't chase the game like that. I didn't have that same ambition as a lot of others in the sense that once I got to a certain period in my career, yeah, that ambition changed, but in high school? I wasn't thinking about being no pro. In college I really wasn't thinking about being a pro. I didn't really start playing until I was 14. I was just loving the game and loved getting 30 points on you. I was in love with playing the game, not what the game could do for me. My first love was that gym! Anyone will tell you that when I was in high school I was a gym rat. For some reason I didn't go to very many parties. I didn't learn or know how to skate, and back then then roller skating was the thang. I wasn't a real good dancer, and back then you had to know how to step. None of that was me. And there was a certain attraction that came with knowing how to do those things. I wasn't into girls back then. It wasn't like I didn't like them. It's not like I was scared, just some guys were a lot more aggressive. Some guys just knew what it took to woo one. If you could dance or skate, man, that was an attraction to both man and woman. Even now my wife loves to dance, and I'll get on the dance floor with her because she likes it. I still can't dance, but I'm cool enough to fake it.

On Friday nights they used to always have a party at the downtown YMCA for youngsters. I'd go sometimes, but my attraction was the gym. I had a deal with the janitor at our school, Mr. Winters, where at night I could shoot around if I swept the floor. So I always stayed late. I'd shoot then sweep the floor. I had a friend, Bobby Chapman, who always wanted to be with me and shoot. So I'd tell him what the janitor told me and I put the job on him. And I can still see Mr. Winter's face because he was that important to me and to my career in helping me get to where I was going. And this is back in 1968. It shows me how important the '60s were to my life. The choices I made kept me out of harm's way because there was always a chance to be in harm's way where I came from. And that janitor gave me a choice, one that I never got a chance to thank him for. But when you're growing up, you just don't know how to say thank you until you get older when you realize what someone did and helped you get to where you are. I'm not even sure if he's alive, but I never got a chance to thank Chapman either.

The other guys I came up with were Jerry Lee and Gary Tyson. I used to spend the night over at Lee's house. He lived off Canton Street and he had like eight or nine brothers and sisters. I was closer to him than, say, King. And Tyson and I played ball all of the time together, including high school, in the summer, and eventually in college. Those were my high school guys. Harold Harris aka "Butch" or "Butch Dog" and I were real close, too. Butch is no longer with me because he ended up having some issues. He needed mental health treatment. So we kind of fell off from one another. But me and Butch Dog used to spend a lot of time together. Anthony Gilkey is another one. Now these were all football guys. I just lost Gilkey. I used to stay over his house in high school, too.

Martin had a big bro we used to call "Big Man." And he's the one who introduced me to jazz music. I listened to Thelonious Monk, Art Blakey, Lee Morgan, Coltrane, Miles, The Crusaders, Lonnie Liston Smith at his house. All of the jazz legends. They played a major role in my young adult life. That became a part of what I listened to throughout my life.

Leslie was one of those guys who would never let anything happen to me. Unfortunately, he's no longer here either. I miss him and all my boys. It's like everything else. Life has its own ways of dealing you cards. Sometimes you don't know how to play the hand, sometimes you get a bad hand. I came up with some great guys. I didn't outgrow them. Some of us just ended up going our separate ways. That bothered me sometimes, too. I always ask myself: *Is there more I coulda done to help?* I do think about it because I'm always compassionate about the guys I came up with. But like everything else, you get older and you move on. There's a history about someone in a group becoming successful and them bringing their people with them, and those people becoming a bad influence. A good example of that not happening is the Wu-Tang Clan. You gotta guy who knew a lot of street guys who got talent and was able to get them to understand there are certain sacrifices in order to be successful as a team. Then you can explode individually, too. It's deep, man. Most times those guys are not willing to make the necessary changes and the sacrifices. That's why I admire LeBron James for how he did it. He asked his boys or told them, "Hey if we gonna hang, you gotta bring something to the table beside you." I missed that. I was close to a lot of guys coming up, and you want to bring all of them with you, but you can't. That's not reality. Most of the times, our guys keep doing the same thing. They see you growing and they stop growing.

* * *

I guess it was my imagination. That's the best way to put it. I imagined someone was guarding me. Then, I'd go to the right. I'd imagine someone guarding me and then I'd go to the left. That's what I did in high school, in the gym. I'd practice against an imaginary defense. I knew the game was designed to be played as a team so I'd imagine another team guarding me. I had that method all the way until I was in the pros. In order to get better, I knew you had to try different things. I was in the backyard shooting hoops at somebody's house one time, and my uncle, my momma's brother, told me something I'll never forget. He said: "Tell me this, George. How many pros use both hands? How many pros can use the opposite hand?"

I wasn't sure of the answer. So I just said, "I don't think that many of 'em."

He said, "You right. They can't because they don't practice it." And then after that he said something that got me: "Most people practice what they can do; they don't practice what they can't." Right then, that light flicked on inside my head. It made so much sense! I understood everything he was saying to me in that moment.

So I started working on it. That way I could lay it up in traffic...with the opposite hand. I could lay it up just as high with the left hand as I could with my right. This was all imagination while I was practicing. I imagined how to put the ball in the hole more than one way. I taught myself how to put that ball in the hole a lot of ways. I had a shot for every defense you put on me because in my mind I'd already seen it, already worked it out. Back then a 230-pounder could put his hands on my 180-pound frame, so I had to figure out a way to be able to use that strength against him. I gotta know how to roll off. I gotta know how the defender pushes me and make that out to be my advantage. I was able to come up with that way back then. That's how my mind was working, which goes back to the educational part. I was able to have defenders push me at an angle where I could shoot a bank shot. That's geometry. I started thinking, *Dang, I ain't ever have to take geometry in class, but I was pretty good at it.* It's all angles. And being able to understand that aspect of the game is how and why I could score. I could stand up and spin the ball off the glass, then I was able to do the same thing in the game. With both hands. In traffic. Imagination. My finger roll, that ain't nothing but imagination. But—before I did it—I saw it already from Wilt Chamberlain, Connie Hawkins, Dr. J. My imagination gave me the chance to perfect it though. I could do it further than any of them did. I did it from different angles, different heights, different distances.

* * *

I wasn't ever scared. I didn't care who I played. I knew I could shoot, I knew I could play. I never asked myself how good I was. I didn't know exactly how good I was, but I knew I wasn't bad. I guess it was how I came up. My brothers—Booker, my oldest brother especially—used to beat me down all of the time. That brotha beat me down. My oldest brother, he was special. He was revered in the city before me. He was in the Curtis Jones era in Detroit. And he was one of those brothas who would never back down. He played both ends of the court, could shoot the ball, guard you, talk stuff. He used to say, "George ain't better than me." He used to say that to Coach Merriweather all the time. He was just that kinda brother.

But once I was able to overcome him and beat him whenever I wanted to, I didn't ever worry about anybody else. That didn't happen until college though. I didn't start beating him regularly until I was at Eastern Michigan when he used to come up and play against me. And after that, I never said he couldn't beat me. I knew I could finally beat him, didn't have to say anything.

I always talk about The Franklin as the place where I built my confidence up. I had some guys before me: Leo Tolman, Larry Middlebrooks, LC Williams, Tweet Williams, Ralph Simpson, Spencer Haywood. I used to watch them and saw how dominant they were. As I got a little older and I got better, thangs changed. It was my turn. I was finishing high school at that time. I had gotten to 6'6" by that time. I was at a new level. When I did play against them, they saw my potential. And that's why I say I was never scared because of who I was playing against and the environment I was doing it in.

Franklin Sullivan was really my workplace. It was basically a training center in our neighborhood in East Detroit. I stayed at my grandmomma's house a lot, and she lived down the street from it. So I was always there. It had a boxing ring in there, and people would run laps around the gym. When I was young, it was the place that became my place to get better. The Franklin also had programs up there. So it served as a community center, too, with programs for kids and programs for adults. So at any age, you could walk up in there, and it had something for you.

I was just recently talking to my guy, Gary Tyson, about how my brother and them dominated the Franklin when we were all younger. And the Franklin was set up where we'd only get to play against them every now and then. The young cats only got on the court if the older guys were one player short, or we were lucky enough to have our little squad up there to call "Next." It was one of the places that if you lost a game, you might not play the rest of the day. So while the older guys were playing, we trained. We worked on different parts of our games and fundamentals: dribbling, conditioning, drills, defensive stances, running. And we'd work on this by ourselves, trying to get ourselves ready for when our time came to play. That's where we got educated. We were young bucks trying to get ourselves ready for our turns while playing against dominant, alpha men who wanted to—and did at times—dominate us.

I played a lot against those older guys. So I had to be mentally tough because they talk so much while beating you down at the same time. They were teaching me while they're beating me down. And Booker, my brother, was one of the biggest trash-talkers in the city. So I even got that when I wasn't at the Franklin. All of them guys, who came up before us, taught us. And after those older players got older and moved on, we took over. That's where I honed my skills. That's where I got it right. And I was there every day. I'd practice there during the week to get ready to play at St. Cecilia's on the weekends. My older brothers dominated there while I was in high school. And as time went by and they'd go on to college, we came in and dominated at Franklin Sullivan.

My reputation, though, comes from St. Cecilia's. They call it the "Motown of basketball." Inside that red brick church gym is where I put on display what I was doing at The Franklin. Both of them have great significance in my career and in my confidence building; both gave me the confidence that I could go anywhere and play. I used to bring my own team to St. Cecilia's, and Sam Washington was running it. For everybody in Detroit, that's where they played on the weekends. From Dave Bing to Magic Johnson and Campy Russell, all the greats came there to play.

St. Cecilia was like the hood alley. Who was in the stands? All the pimps, hustlers, gamblers. There was only one side for the crowd. It was Cracker Jack box small, and everyone was yelling at you to let you know whether you could play or not. When I became a young pro, still a teenager, I used to go in there and play, but I couldn't get in. Too packed. People filled up on the one side. The out-of-bounds line had people standing on it all of the way around the gym. And if you touched one of them, you were out of bounds because they were on the line. That's how big St. Cecilia's was for us. And that's where I got my rep. They say I built it. If anyone talks about St. Cecilia's, mostly they'll talk about me.

Yet, I had no understanding of the foundation I was laying down. I was just hoopin'. But that's always been me. I hoop. I came to entertain and I brought my own crew. I'm the same way today: I only hang out with my circle. Some have died along the way, but I gotta circle that I don't let anyone else in. And that's how it was back then when we played. I brought my own team. You know how back in the day everybody had their little team? Well, I had my own. There was a showdown: me vs. Russell. I can't remember how many I got, around 40 or 50 points, but the next week, Russell wanted to play with us. That's no disrespect to Russell because Russell could play. But at the high school/college level—even more than when I was a pro—I could flat out play. I had a passion for the game, man. I loved to practice, I was zoned in. And I accepted all challenges. I played against pros like Willie Norwood and them. He tried to hit me with an elbow when I tried to shot fake him. Yeah, well he tried to hit me with that move while putting his elbow in my face! I ducked out of the way. I was like, *Dang, this brotha tried to hurt me. Is that what we doin' out here?*

St. Cecilia helped me figure out that I could play ball anywhere. That's how treacherous the league was back then. There's always that crew who thinks they can play but didn't make it, so they come to St. Cecilia's to make their name off you. I grew up with nothing but guys like that. I had a reputation so I always had that to deal with. And I accepted it. I took those challenges and comers. I wasn't ever scared, always had a posse with me. A posse that wouldn't let anyone do anything to me. I was very well protected. I think that, too, was an advantage for me. I never had a fight. If somebody got too close to me, guys would get them off me. There weren't guns and stuff like there are today. It was just hands back then.

I was real little and skinny. You hit me too hard on the court, someone might come out on the floor. That's the kinda love my guys and I had with one another, which led me to have a wonderful relationship with them. That's also the same kinda love I have for St. Cecilia's. I went over there in the summer of 2021 when I was in Detroit just to take a look at it while we were shooting my documentary back in the hood. We had a chance to talk about it. That gym is a big part of my history. I was 17 or 18 years old when I stepped into that gym. You had to earn your way to play at St. Cecilia's. I ain't gonna say

I was the best ever to come outta there; that wouldn't be fair and that's not who I am. But I know I was one of them.

Haywood coached me when he came back home to Detroit from the 1968 Olympics in AAU. He went around the city asking, "Who can I coach to have me an AAU team? Who's the best 15-year olds?" When people told him it was me, he came over to see me play at the Franklin and told me he's putting an AAU team together. I told him that I'd play. Then he got Bubba Hawkins. Then he went and got seven or eight more guys. Hawkins could hoop. He was one of those top named players in high school. And years later he ended up being my brother-in-law. Hawkins and I both averaged more than 30 points apiece on that team. And we never lost.

So right before we went to the state tournament, the team that we beat turned us in. I was 15 years old, but you had to be 15 years old at a certain time, and they said I turned 15 too early, so they disqualified us. I went home and told my mom that they said I was too old and I tried to get anything I could to say that I turned 15 at the right time. It didn't work. Broke my little heart. And I didn't know any better. Haywood had asked if I was 15 and said we were playing against other 15 year olds in a 15-and-under league, and I was 15. But we were too good. If we were losing, no one would have cared. But we beat everybody. All over the city. Man, Haywood and I still talk about that story. That's what they call street cred. That ain't media. That ain't the NBA, college. That's street. And that's who I played for. They were the first people who appreciated what I was doing with that ball. And that meant the world to me. Still does today.

We went from alley-to-alley playing. That's how we grew up in east Detroit. We used to play on a tire rim, which was smaller in size than a normal rim. We played with what we had. Tire rims, spoke rims, no nets. That small rim aspect became a reality as I got older. When in practice they'd put a small rim on top of the big rim, that made you shoot with more of an arch because unless you learned how to shoot with an arch the ball wasn't going in the rim. You couldn't shoot a line drive. And if you look at the great shooters today, they all shoot with an arch. I call them "one-piece jump shots." You jump up with the ball in your hand like a serving tray, and before you get to the top of your jump, the ball is gone. That's how I learned how to shoot as a kid because I wasn't as big or strong. So because of that tiny rim, I was able to learn to use my legs to be able to be that spring and use my wrist to be that flicker. That's how you get that arch on it. You could shoot it farther and use more of your shoulders. Everything, I figured out, starts with the legs, then shoulder, and ends with the wrist. Legs, shoulder, wrist. One-piece jumper. We used to put those rims on those telephone polls and just shoot. That was our reality.

CHAPTER FOUR

THE INCIDENT

How easy is it to lose everything when you lose yourself?

A lot of people are in jail for not being able to control their emotions. We have emotional disorders; that's what mental health issues are. We have those moments where you wish you could take something back. Our jails are full of people who wish they could take something back, take that moment in their lives back. When I hit Jay Piccola in college, I snapped. I went blank. I went dark. All I could think of is being mistreated and reacting. And that cost me my college career.

I got upset. Things weren't going my way. It was an NCAA College Division national semifinals game. It was my sophomore season at Eastern Michigan. My freshman year—the NCAA had finally allowed freshmen to play varsity sports—I was establishing myself, averaging 17 to 18 points a game. My sophomore year I was averaging almost 30. We were playing this team from Roanoke College in Virginia. The Maroons. I felt they were cheating. I felt that I was being taken advantage of. I looked at the environment we were in. Being in Evansville, Indiana, I started looking at the prejudice, which was already all stored up anyway. I was scoring, had more than 20 at the half, but we we losing by double digits in a game we were supposed to win. And then the incident happened.

Before I even threw the punch, they threw me out of the game because of a scuffle—if you wanna call it that—over a rebound between Piccola and me. So I was frustrated. They ejected me from the game because of that scuffle. So then I was on the sidelines. Then the same guy, Piccola, came over to me. I didn't know if he was shaking my hand or what, but my mind was in another place, and all I saw was him, and he was the one who was beating me. So I raised up and hit him.

I hit the brotha so hard I knocked him completely out. And by him laying on that floor and me seeing him on that floor, I wanted to hit him again, but he didn't get back up. Then I started seeing his eyes buckling. It scared the life out of me. The rest of my guys started fighting, too. It started a brawl. It was jam-packed in that arena. They started throwing stuff at me. I had to have the police escort me out to the locker room. I was dealing with all of this and I was still a kid. Still a teenager at 18. Fortunately, Piccola was alright. But then I started thinking about all the things I would give up: All-American status, Pan-Am Games, Olympics. And all I could think was: *I created that because I lost my emotions.* I lost myself. And I said from then on: *I'm not going to let anything put me in a spot to where I can be in this situation again.*

My coach at the time, Jim Dutcher, at some point got on the microphone in the arena trying to settle the people down and said, "The players who got involved in this, they will never play for me again."

I was in the locker room, so I didn't hear it, but my teammates told me. And since that was the first game of a division semifinals, we had another game to play after that. Roanoke ended up beating us so we played in the consolation game. Obviously, I didn't play. I got on a plane and I went back to Eastern. Two or three of the other guys did the same thing because they were mad at the coach. When I got back, the athletic director told me, "Hey, man, we're suspending you for *next* year. We also don't know if you'll be able to play your senior year."

I said, "What?"

It was my sophomore year, and I was averaging 29.5 points a game as one of the top scorers in the nation. After they told me about the pending suspension, I withdrew from school. I didn't just quit; I withdrew. I at least had enough sense to not just walk away. I went through the procedures.

I never made a lot of bad choices when I was young. And those that I did make I was able to recover from. They became teaching tools. That was my first incident. Because of it I knew there was no coming back once I left. I couldn't play ball anymore. My college career was over. I caused it. It was all on me. When they threw me out of the game, I coulda sat back, never thrown that punch, and let my boys win it. But it didn't work out like that. And that was the beginning of my journey into getting to where I got. I honestly think that's when I became "Ice." I learned from that situation how you can't lose your composure or your cool just because something isn't going right for you. Know that you can't get caught up to where the situation can kill you or take your freedom away.

How easy is it to lose everything when you lose yourself?

When I looked in the mirror right after that incident all I saw was a scared little kid who didn't know what was going to happen. I knew that there were consequences for what I had done that hadn't been addressed yet. So I was scared. And when I got the news, it terrified me. I was in shock. That's when sorry is too late. You can't take that moment back. It's like a lot of us in life. We react instead of thinking first. Life is a competition, most times with yourself. That force blinds you, makes you greedy, makes you boisterous, makes you think it's all about you, makes you forget that gift and where you got it from. That's the competition aspect of what I'm talking about, the one we struggle with. I always go back to the first competition—and people think I'm crazy when I say this—but the first competition that ever existed in our understanding is when the devil tried to compete against, who I call, Jehovah God. From God's point of view, we know that He could have just cut the devil out and shut him out right there and never had to deal with it anymore. But in reality there were a lot of other beings around that saw the question and felt that they had to prove the difference. And that's that choice again, that choice that we as human beings have to make. You can follow this or you can follow that. That bad spirit is always trying to interfere with that positive spirit. People don't realize how powerful the force out here is.

Anyhow, I wrote Piccola a letter of apology. He read the letter in my documentary and he said, "It's about to bring me to tears." That's so meaningful. In the early part of my life, to me that incident was one of my biggest letdowns, just dealing with that. So when I wanted to do the documentary, I told the producers that story and how that moment changed my life. They wanted to feature it.

Piccola wound up becoming the president of Puma. And I was told he used to carry around a George Gervin bobblehead. All the guys used to say, "George, man, everywhere Jay used to go, he'd carry your bobblehead and say, 'This guy here, he's a character!'"

When he used to go out and do a speech or a presentation, he'd put my bobblehead on the table and say, "I brought a friend with me. He just can't talk." And Piccola's a character, too. He had personality. It seemed like the employees loved him. And I could see why they loved him. He helped Puma become a multi-million dollar company. It's interesting to think the impact that situation had an effect on both of our lives. It blows my mind.

Piccola knows me now. He appreciates my humility not only about what I was able to accomplish in my professional career, but also who I've become as a human being. I think that's what he admired over the years about me the most. It meant a lot to me to get Piccola in the film. I didn't want to run away from the incident. I also had no idea it was going to turn out the way that it did. To hear him talk, to hear how humble he was and he's become, to hear how me going to his retirement in 2017 in Boston and me speaking at his retirement—he didn't even know I was coming—moved him. When they asked me to come and be a part of his retirement, I said to him during my speech, "You know I am so glad that I finally have the chance to tell you 'I'm sorry.'" We embraced and hugged.

I later asked him to be in the documentary, and he said, "George, I'd love to." That how deep that was.

In life it really all comes back to how you dealt with it. I mean, I've tried my whole life not to be ugly to people. I just can't put my finger on why things in my life have come full circle like that. I know where I am spiritually. So I know when you have a spiritual appetite, these are parts of the spiritual food you get.

CHAPTER FIVE

THE SHOT

And we're in a gym…

When I left Eastern Michigan, I went to Pontiac, Michigan, to play for a semi-pro team called the Chaparrals. We played two games on the weekends. I got paid $500 every weekend while playing for a brotha named Roy Washington. And he got me a car so that I could make the games. That car was a Riviera. Emerald green. Beige interior. Big ol' 8-track. It was nice. And this was in the Continental League, so I was playing against older men. I'm not going to say the Continental League was a bunch of has-beens; it was a bunch of guys who had their turn, and they were like me: coming from bad situations—they got hurt, bad timing, etc.—but they still loved the game, too.

And I was the young buck. They couldn't catch me back then. I played with them about six or seven months. I was playing well, averaging 30-plus points a game, and Johnny "Red" Kerr saw me. It was after a game against a Flint, Michigan, team led by Justin Thigpen. It was a good game. He and I battled. He was averaging 38 points per game, so he was a bad boy, too. I didn't know Kerr from the next man on the moon. I don't remember the conversation I had with Kerr, but somehow Sonny Vaccaro came into the picture, too. I met Vaccaro through Jackson Nunn, one of the football players I went to Eastern with. He introduced me to Vaccaro around 1972 when Vaccaro had the Dapper Dan Roundball Classic. Vaccaro came to meet Coach Merriweather at Merriweather's house in Detroit. That's how they hooked up. According to Vaccaro, Nunn reached out to him to help me because of what happened to me at Eastern. Vaccaro apparently had helped Nunn when he was having problems getting noticed and getting a scholarship to college. He was part of the reason Nunn ended up at Eastern. Still to this day, I don't know why Vaccaro was interested in me. Vaccaro wasn't an agent. I don't know where he came from. Somehow, he had a friendship with Al Bianchi, who was then the Virginia Squires coach. From what I was told, Vaccaro made a call, and the next thing I knew, we're in Virginia.

Vaccaro, Merriweather, and I were in a gym in the Norfolk Scope Arena. Merriweather was talking to Earl Foreman, the owner of the Squires, and Coach Bianchi was up in the stands. And they didn't know me. They took the word of Kerr who told them they needed to see me. I don't think Kerr was even in the gym at all that day. He wasn't even the scout for them. He was their business manager, but I think he had seen me play and knew where I'd fit in—and that was the ABA. I think he just told Foreman to meet me.

And all I remember is they told me to start shooting. It was just me and a few kids on the court who were tossing the balls back to me. I had been warming up already, so when they wanted me to shoot, I started droppin' 'em. Vaccaro has said that I hit 50 shots in a row, and I was shooting in my street shoes! But I don't remember that. Knowing me, I ain't gonna do that. I'm not shooting in my gators. But that's what Vaccaro says. I don't know if he's embellishing it, but I do know that I made a lot of shots whatever I was wearing. Keep in mind I never thought about being a pro. I was pretty content with what I was doing. I was in love with Joyce, I got the game, I got a few bucks, I got a ride, and I'm rollin'. But back then, like Kerr said: I could flat-out score. And I loved that about myself. They said I shot 30 to 35 times, and I made 30 out of 35 or 30 out of 30. But whatever the number was, I heard someone say, "That's good." And I stopped shooting right then. After that someone instantly said: "We'll take him."

They signed me to a contract. We went into trainer Bob Travaglini's little office and signed the deal on a paper napkin. At the time they were losing Charlie Scott, who was a special player. I'm glad he got into the Hall of Fame. So again for me this was being in the right place at the right time. Scott was playing for the Squires before I came and I never got a chance to play with him. He went on to the NBA at midseason to the Phoenix Suns. And Scott was big for the Squires. He was like Julius Erving, who was already on the Squires. When I went into their front offices, they had a big picture of Scott on the wall. And I think that's part of why they were looking at me. Dr. J was right. He said I might be the only person in the history of basketball to literally shoot for his contract, and I did.

I was in the pros and not college 'cause I made a mistake. I realized that I did 'cause that wasn't me. I didn't have any real anxieties after that because I knew I wasn't a bad guy or this and that. I made a choice, I withdrew from school, and I moved on. I never looked at where the game would take me because I was just in the moment. Being older and looking back, I wonder: *was that good or bad?* I don't know. I wouldn't ask anyone else to go through it like that. I educated myself to know that I was lucky. The fact that I was still able to play—and even at a higher level—was very fortunate.

And once I got out of school, Joyce was still with me most of the time. She traveled with me during those semi-pro games. I was driving up there in that Riveria to her dorm in Eastern Michigan because she was still in school. She didn't get out of school until I became a pro. She was the support I had during that time. She was my girl and she was a good one. And that was a learning process for me of how to take care of her.

I was pretty much an unknown. Eastern Michigan isn't a big school, and at the time all of the attention in college was going to Bill Walton and UCLA and Bob McAdoo at

North Carolina. Once you were out of school, you lost any publicity. The only publicity I was getting was how to knock a brotha out. I wasn't in school and I was playing against the hood. During the semi-pro days, I used to go to the prisons to play. But Merriweather knew how good I was, and once we got to Virginia, others found out. I went from making $500 a weekend as a semi-pro to $50,000 a year on the Squires. Three years, $150,000 was the contract with a $4,000 signing bonus, and I came in at midseason. I was like, *Where do I sign?*

But more than the money, I was just appreciative to have an opportunity. You gotta remember less than a year ago I was in a locker room in Evansville, Indiana, wondering if I was *ever* going to have any basketball career. And now I'm considered a professional basketball player. And once I was on the team, getting this money, my goal was to show them that I was worthy of this. And that wasn't easy. I mean, it was easy once I played. Once I got on the floor, they were all like, "Oh, he can play. He can play." But once they saw I could play, that's when they started to test the other parts of me: my mentality, my heart. They wanted to find out what I was made of. *Can he take a punch? If someone hits him, will he quit? How can I get to him?* All a part of the game.

Merriweather stayed with me for a while in Virginia until I got settled and then he went back to Detroit. He made sure I got my apartment and stuff, made sure I was good and then he left me with Dr. J and Fatty Taylor, who both became mentors. Merriweather was telling the people with the Squires, "You know George can shoot better than Doc." Itching them on.

I was on my own really for the first time. First time having my own apartment, first time making my own decisions, paying the bills. That was a big change for me, but the game was still easy. Because I was still a student of the game. Came early, stayed late. I was getting to know the guys that I'm teaming with. Fatty's family kinda took me in. He and his wife, Janice, had little kids, and I used to spend time over there with them. Things all worked out. Then Doc left. Then from there it pretty much became Ice.

* * *

This is where the cars come in and the roles they've played. First the Riviera. Then the 225, Deuce and a Quarter. Then I got the Cadillac. My first one. I got it when I turned pro. Triple black. Drop top Eldorado with the Rolls Royce grill in the front. I wish I still had a picture of that car. I couldn't wait for the season to be over so that I could go home and drive it back to Detroit. Detroit is known for cars; we are the car capital of America. All of the cars come from there, so cars are a big deal. And I'm an inner-city Detroit guy, not one of those guys from the suburbs of Detroit, and a lot of what we saw that impressed us, especially in that era, was all of the different kinds of cars. You had Superfly and all of them. He had the big Lincoln Continental with the big grill on it and the big peace signs over the headlights. That impressed and influenced me. So when I got money and went to the car showroom, I was like, "Oh yeah, I want that."

And this was the '70s so a nice car wasn't but about $20,000 or so. But for my personality, that really wasn't me. It was more of the environment that influenced me because I really didn't like that kind of attention. But I liked style, and the style was good! It not only brought the girls—and I wasn't married at the time, but that didn't stop them from being attracted to the car even when I was—but also the guys always wanting to ride, and the police always wanting to check you out, all of that. And I got stopped a lot in that car. I'm dressed sharp, got the hats on, and the cops are like, "Let's see who this brotha is." So I looked at it one way as being a part of my personality. But the car got torn up after I left Joyce's house one day. A Volkswagen hit me so hard that it spun the whole car around and bent the frame. After that I got rid of it.

I'd had that car for a couple of years, but that car was the beginning of another kind of learning for me. It tells a lot about how I came up. Single parent. Probably if I had a dad,

I would have had a different perspective on the real value of something like that. Me being a dad now, I'd say to my own son, Gee, if he was going to go down that route, "Well, son, you know that car there you might attract more than what you want." I would have the influence to say, "Yeah, son, it looks good, but let's think about this."

That's what I didn't really have and that's how the whole car situation with me became a learning tool. The lesson of the car became more important than the car itself. That everything that glitters ain't gold lesson because my mom didn't really know what I liked when I was that age. She was too busy being the lion of the family, protecting us, so I never got that lesson until I went through it. And here I was: a young pro, making $50,000 to $60,000—money I'd never seen in my life. I could pretty much buy anything I wanted in those days. And at 19 years old, I only knew so much. And the sad part is that the same thing is still happening today. Look at some of these guys out here. Now they can afford 10 cars, but they probably got 11. It's the environment. I also learned you can only drive one at a time. And if you don't have someone managing 'em, you probably don't know which ones have gas in them. That was all a part of me growing up. And I loved it. I can't deny that. I was livin' on the scene with a gangster lean. Yet, there was nothing gangster about me.

CHAPTER SIX

COOL

You can throw "cool" on it, but for me it was just life.

People always tell me, "Man, Ice, you, just so...cool." And I always say: "I ain't tryin' to be cool, I ain't gotta script on what is cool. I'm just tryin' to be me." By understanding myself and being comfortable with myself, I never felt the weight of trying to act a certain way, you know? I can't act any other way because that's when it becomes a role, I never played a role. Even within the game, I was just out playing ball, hoopin'. I never knew any other way to be. That's how I approached my game and life.

I really never understood what "cool" was. Well, obviously I did with *The Mack* and all of the other movies we grew up on, but that was acting cool. He was playing a role. From the outside people were looking at me as being cool, but I was just being myself. I mean, I'm from Detroit so how I dress and present myself is from my environment and how I grew up. Back then, I always wore gators, lizards, always wore the exotic shoes. Kept a Borsalino hat. I used to wear those Parker of Vienna sweaters with a tie. C'mon man, that's style. But it also represented where I was from and the times we came up in. Places like Chicago, Detroit, we all dressed up. That was part of how I was raised, and that's what I saw, and to me that looked good. So if you want to, you can throw "cool" on it, but for me that was just life.

They called me "Ice" and all that, but that was just a title to me. That wasn't my persona, even though after the incident at Eastern Michigan, my demeanor was calm. I was chill about almost everything because I refused to let anything bother me like that ever again. But cool wasn't how I was trying to act. If the things that I did came off as cool, that's great. But I wasn't trying to be cool. I always was natural or honest about anything I did or who I was.

But being cool was more like a way of life then. In Detroit you saw it all of the time. Like a lot of other major cities, Detroit had its own cool with the superstars and just cats walking downtown and in our neighborhoods. The Temptations were cool, Smokey Robinson was cool, Marvin Gaye was cool, so were some of the older guys I'd see when I'd be going to hoop. The men who would come to the family picnics and to the house parties. The hustlers, the pimps, the bus drivers, the businessmen once they got off work. We were all trying to emulate them, trying to emulate each other.

If you ask me about cool, though, Coach Merriweather was cool to me. The epitome of it. Just his style, how he dressed, how he dealt with us. To us he was one of the James Bond kinda guys. Merriweather didn't wear suits; he wore sport coats. He had all of the gadgets. The watch, the pin gun. He always drove something nice, and the ladies liked him. He made out pretty well. He's just a great dude. Smart, educated, military background, and had street sense. He's always been mature and a no-nonsense kind of guy, one of those guys who never backed down. You wanna fight, he'd say, "Okay." Always prepared for a fight. And he didn't stop his job in the school system in Detroit once I became pro. He stayed in education for my whole playing career until he retired. But he had a lot of other relationships, too. He was an agent for William Bedford and Shawn Kemp. He had a relationship with Dominque Wilkins. He made some great contacts, was an advisor for a lot of people. And he was always around for me when I made decisions to hire people and make major decisions—except when it came to martial advice. I kid him because Merriweather has been married like four times. He wasn't the one to talk to. But he was influential to me. Especially in things I defined as being cool.

The other side of cool is not only the things that you have or how you carry yourself, but also how you handle situations. If you handle things peacefully, most times they will work out for you. That was a part of my DNA, which became another lesson. If you can recognize problems, okay. Now that you've recognized what the problem is let's find a solution to fix it. We can argue about problems all of the time, but if we don't try to find a solution, the problem's still there. So arguing and all that about a situation and not finding a solution to fix the problem never made sense to me. That's basically been my mentality throughout my life.

There's no one cooler than Ice Cube. I'm coaching in his BIG3, the three-on-three basketball tournament. They call it a league, but I call it more of a tournament because it takes place over only eight weeks, not including the playoffs, and we only play six-to-eight games depending on your win-loss record, which to me is more like a tournament. My team is the Ghost Ballers. We got some good players, but what I love most is being able to talk to the young guys about life.

This last season the BIG3 had it's first All-Star Game. Dr. J and I were selected as coaches for the All-Star Game. I felt I had the best team, but I was a little disappointed because three of my players didn't show up for practice for the game. So I told the ones who did show up that they'd be the ones starting in the All-Star Game. Now, from my perspective, the All-Star Game is supposed to be a special thing. At the end of the year, you are one of the 12 guys picked to represent the league, a league you chose to be in. So once I decided to start the ones who showed up, it wasn't about the game anymore. If you act like, "Well, I'm gonna show up when I want to," well, not on me you won't. And I don't have to sit up and argue with you or explain myself. My sentiment was: "You might've led the BIG3 in scoring, but I led the *big league* in scoring four times! So, don't get it twisted."

I'm the wrong guy to disrespect. But I'm also the same guy who you can learn something from if you want. And this maybe where sometimes the perception of being cool comes into it because of my reaction. I really didn't care if one or two of the players may have been pissed. To me the game itself is recreation, but the league is something Cube put together for the players to stay on stage and make a little money. You gotta respect that. This man done put up all this money to create this opportunity for the players, and that is how they were gonna treat it? I'm not going to yell and scream or disrespect anyone to make them understand that, but in my own way, I'm going to do what I feel is right to make sure a certain level of respect remains.

We live and we learn. And preferably you live long enough to help somebody else out along the way. No matter how hard the lesson. And for coaching that's when it's more than basketball for that coach. That's one of the things I learned from coaching in the ABA in 2000. I coached a team called the Detroit Dogs. I had a bunch of inner-city players. I knew it was very important to tell them in the beginning, "Look here, if I get on you, I'm not getting on you personally. I'm getting on your basketball character." I wanted them to understand that this isn't personal. Most of the times, they bought into it, and I didn't have any issues. I was being upfront with them.

Same thing in the BIG3. I told them, "Look here, this is 3-on-3. We grew up playing 3-on-3. If you forgot that, we not going to win any games. I ain't coaching, I'm just taking you out when you get tired." It's a cool thing Cube is doing. I feel it's part of my responsibility to make sure those, who are involved with it, respect that. I'm glad he called me to be a part of it. And we really didn't know each other before this. We only really knew *of* each other. I remember I'd just got finished working out with Merriweather and got a text: "Hey Ice, it's Cube. I got something I wanna talk to you about."

I texted him back, "Who is this?"

He texted, "Cube."

Then I texted, "Call me."

He immediately called and said, "Ice, I'm doing this league called the 'BIG3' and I want you to be a part of it."

I said, "Cool, Cube. If you're going to do it, I'll do it with you."

Notice I call him "Cube," not "Ice Cube." I told him, "I'm older. I was Ice first."

* * *

When I played my approach was slow is quick. I'd slowly set you up then quickly go by you. That was my philosophy. Set-ups are always slow. If I had the ball, the defender was always going to go for the fake because he wanted the ball. So I'd slowly fake him, and they'd slowly go for the fake. I've had people say to me, "Ice, it always looks like you were playing in slow motion."

But I wasn't. I'd say to them, "Think about this: you ever been on a TGV train? Like the one over in France? It can get up to almost 200 miles an hour, but when you look out the window while you're on it, it looks like you are passing everything up slowly." Same concept to how I played, same concept as looking up in the sky at a plane. The plane is actually moving hundreds of miles per hour, but from the ground, from 10,000 feet away, it looks like it's moving slowly. I was going a 100 miles an hour on the court. It looked like I was moving slow, but the guy guarding me was behind me. There was an art to it. Many people saw that and looked at it as art, and it was. Strictly art.

Alex English was sort of the same way, but he didn't do his with style. He just got it done. No flair, no flavor. No excitement to it, but once it got done, you'd look up and be like, *That brotha got 30?* He got 2,000 points eight years in a row. Unheard of. But what separated us was I did it a different way. I made the people go Ooh and Ahh, and English made people go to sleep. (I'm just razzin' you, Alex.) But when you woke up, you'd realize we'd done the same thing. Just in different ways. But because of the style I had to the way I played, people embraced it differently. They attached it to my personality and who they felt I was. That flair made it art.

People associate part of that coolness in my game not only because of the style I played with, but also with the fact that most of the time while I was playing, I was always smiling. Everyone who played against me knew that I loved the game. They knew I loved it. Michael Cooper said it best, "Ice is going to be known as the coolest player to ever play because he played with a passion." That was the joy I got from playing. It was fun to me. I was an entertainer, I was a scorer. The game was me. I put myself into it when I played. And that's the cool that came out of it.

CHAPTER SEVEN

ABA

We were a word-of-mouth league.

No. 21. That was my first number for the Virginia Squires. I have seen some old pictures of me in it, so I did at one time have No. 21 on, but I don't remember ever playing a game in it. And I don't remember how I got 44. I can't remember if I chose it or if they gave it to me. But once I became 44, I always used to tell Reggie Jackson, "I wore No. 44 because of you!" And I used to see him before I became a young pro because he was in Arizona at that time at Arizona State and I was at Mesa Junior College. As we got older, we got to know one another pretty well. I used to go spend time with him in Monterey, California, on that five-acre ranch; went to that amazing warehouse, where all of his cars were; and played in his golf tournament he used to have at Pebble Beach.

But he was No. 44—and so was Jerry West. So was one of my heroes from Detroit, Ralph Simpson. Them some bad boys there! And Marvin Gaye. He died at 44 years old. Gaye and I used to talk about 44. We shared a connection through that number. Gaye didn't have any reason to look up to me. I was just a ballplayer, but we were still two artists. Even the first Black president of the United States happened to be the 44th one. It's to the point that if I get a golf cart at the golf club to play golf with my guys and the cart number is 44, they all get scared. They're like, "Ah, naw, he got 44, he can't go wrong." I just laugh. Maybe there was some deeper connection to 44. Or maybe Gaye knew something that I didn't.

I used to spend some time with Gaye when I'd come into Los Angeles for games. He'd pick me up, and we'd just go to the studio. I was there when he was mixing songs for *Here, My Dear*, the album he did for his wife Anna. When he was making "Anna's Song" and "Sparrow," I was right there with him.

One day Gaye's sister came by, got me, and took me to his house. We were playing the Los Angeles Lakers at The Forum, and my boys and I had a hotel room across the street so we could just walk over after the game. I got that knock on the door. I had no idea why she came to get me, but once I got to the house, I knew why. She said, "George, I'm Marvin's sister. I need you to come over and see Marvin."

I could see it in her eyes, the look on her face. Marvin just needed someone who had some sort of understanding of what he was going through. For whatever reason his sister came to me. She knew he was going through it, dealing with those mental health issues. Being a celebrity and stuff, dealing with those outside demons that come with fame—or those that come when you are gifted and exceptional at something—well, life can be dark. Life wears and tears on you. Gaye and I sat in his room for a while and talked while he was in the bed. It was in the same house that his father shot him. We laughed and all that and were getting a little loud, and his sister came in and kind of whispered, "Keep it down because you know Dad's in there with them guns."

That's when I said, "Come on, man, let's get up, go out." Now I ain't never been a club person, but I said, "I'll go out for you." And we went to one of his girl's houses, and he was playing me all of his music I'd never heard before. We ended up staying over there listening until about five in the morning.

And that was the last time I saw him. It was within the next few weeks that his father shot him.

* * *

Dr. J and I used to play one-on-one after practice all of the time my rookie year. That brotha got me right; I was his rookie. After practice he used to be like, "Hey Rook, where you goin'?"

And I'd be like, "Man, I'm about to go get me something to eat."

And Doc'd be like, "Naw, we ain't done yet." And he'd go get that ball. I'll never forget that. I love him for that. He put me under his wing, I used to hang with him. He'd talk to me, and that brotha grew to say about me, "Wow, man." And that's a beautiful thing to hear from someone who helped get you to what you became. When we started he would dunk on me, put moves on me, go by me all types of ways when we would play. I was nervous! I ain't afraid to tell anybody. I mean, I'm playing against the great Julius Erving. And then a week, two weeks went by, and I'd figured out some things. I started shooting that jumper, and the whole thing changed. But I'll never forget what he did to build up my confidence. That self-esteem. After playing one-on-ones against Doc, I knew I could do it.

I played my first game, which was in the Richmond Coliseum, my rookie year. I had 20 points. And Fatty Taylor said to me, "Man, you hooped." And I did what I could to stay on the floor. I remember when Doc got on the *Tonight Show Starring Johnny Carson* that year, and Carson asked him who was one of his favorite players and he said, "George Gervin."

And Carson said, "*Who?*" I just laughed. I never forgot that. I fell in love with Doc even more after that.

What bothered me my rookie year was Al Bianchi was one of those guys who wouldn't play rookies. One game he put me in when we were down against the Utah Stars, and I was bringing us back, but that brotha still didn't play me again for eight, nine, 10 games. That started working on my mentality. So I asked Fatty why Coach Bianchi wasn't playing me. Fatty said, "I don't know why either."

Fatty used to go and talk to Bianchi and ask him, "Coach, why don't you play that man? Why won't you play Ice? He ready." Fatty advocated for me. Fatty was the leader. He was our leader during my era there. It wasn't Doc. The whole time I never said anything, never whined. Well, I whined to myself but not to him. I just stayed in the gym, working. I stayed sharp, ready because I knew my turn was going to come. I was still a pro. Never lost sight of that. And I was still getting paid. Even if he ain't playing me. That was on him. But he was in charge, and I've always respected authority. Yeah, I was in a new system, but it's still the same thing, still gotta apply the lessons from my upbringing. Again, it's how you handle things. And it worked out for me because in my mind I handled it peacefully.

I went from playing 23 minutes a game that rookie year to 35 in my second year. My average went from 14 points a game to 25. I'd gotten settled in. I got to see other players, knew what they could do, knew what I could do. Some guys come in trying to be a star; I never tried to come in and be a star. I came in to be a rookie. And I liked being a rookie. I think that helped me. All those traditions of being a rook—going to get donuts, carrying all of the bags, being the first one to do this or that—those rituals kept me humble.

I also learned that people tend to appreciate you once you wait your turn. And I waited my turn. So once that rookie half-season was over, I had a whole summer. I went home, got my accolades from all of the college guys, and that helped build my confidence and self-esteem up. Then I was looking forward to the next year. I got all of that other stuff behind me. I knew I had a chance to play a whole 84 games plus a preseason. So I was starting out fresh. Plus, I had Doc as my teammate. All of that was exciting for me. Then two months before the season started, they traded Doc to the New York Nets.

When Doc was traded, it opened the door for me. I hated to lose Doc, but Fatty kept encouraging me, saying, "Man, you just as good as Doc." And I never ever looked at it like that. I always looked at it as Doc was in a league of his own. I never compared myself to him. The trade worked out career-wise for both of us. It allowed Doc to take advantage of his skills and it gave me an opportunity. It was almost like I was the next in line. Once again it was being in the right place at the right time. And once I got more minutes on the court with Doc gone, I just looked at it as I got more time to produce. And I did. That's it. Nothing more. I never thought about it like, *Now I'm gonna be The Man*. I was still only 21 years old.

All the while Fatty was still in my ear. When we were traveling to play the Nets in October, I was on the plane sitting next to Fatty and I said, "Dang, I gotta go up against Doc."

And he was like, "What you mean? Doc gotta go up against *you*!" That's how Fatty was talking to me, pushing all my buttons. "You can do what you've been doing on everyone else on Doc." I didn't see that, but he did. Understand, though, Doc was my hero, and I was playing against my hero. Even with all of the one-on-ones we used to play, this was different. I don't remember a lot about the first time we played, but we lost, and I put up good numbers (43 points). Doc got his usual numbers because he always did, and Fatty came up to me and said: "Told you."

After that game and playing so well against Doc, I really thought I was on my way. It reminded me of back in the day when I played against my oldest brother and I'd gotten to a place in my game where he couldn't beat me no matter what he did. It took me mentally to that next level. Doc was that next phase. At mid-season in January, I was put on the cover of *The Sporting News*. "Red-Hot Iceman" it said. To everyone it was like I'd arrived. As a young pro in my second year, I was thrilled, but I don't think I took it any further than that. I didn't go around saying, "Hey, look, I'm on the cover of *The Sporting News*!" I never really got pumped up about any of that stuff. I just kept it moving.

* * *

It wasn't until after I was gone that I realized how much financial trouble the Virginia Squires were in. Unlike a lot of other players, I didn't have any problems getting my checks or anything, but after I left, guys were getting their checks and running to the bank the same day. We were on the road in Utah, probably about 50 games into the season, when I found out. Irwin Weiner, who was my agent and also Dr. J's at the time, called me and said, "Don't play in the game. You've been traded to the San Antonio Spurs."

This was the same time or right after *The Sporting News* cover. It was almost like a jinx. Back then, of course, we didn't have Instagram or Twitter or anything like that, so I got a telegram from the Spurs before the game in Utah saying that I am "now property of the San Antonio Spurs." So I was asking Weiner about this telegram, and he's like, "Yeah, we made the trade. The Spurs bought your contract out from the Virginia Squires, so you're headed to the Spurs, and I'm going to get you on a plane to San Antonio." So I didn't play that game. No one said anything about how much money it was. I didn't know what was going on. All I was doing was following directions.

When I got to San Antonio, I got sent to the Hilton hotel. That was my new home. Once I got there, that's when I found out that the Squires sold my contract to the Spurs for $225,000. After that Earl Foreman, the owner of the

Squires, wanted to renege on the deal. The Spurs and their owner, Angelo Drossos, weren't going for it. So it went to court. I sat in San Antonio for like a month, couldn't play, couldn't practice with them, couldn't go to the practice facility, couldn't have any affiliation with the team. Not until the court case was settled. So Bird Averitt used to come over and get me, and I used to shoot around with him. We played in all types of gyms in the San Antonio area, any place we could find. He hung with me until the trial was over and I officially became a Spur. He was around my age, so we connected. We were just two young bucks. He came out of Pepperdine after he'd just led the nation in scoring in 1973. And Averitt could put up buckets. There wasn't a shot he didn't love. We scored differently. I was probably more accurate in my shot selection than he was. He was from a little bitty town in Kentucky called Hopkinsville. We're talking about the deep part of Kentucky. Grandma and them.

This whole thing took place at the beginning of 1974 and dragged on probably for a shorter amount of time than it actually felt to me. But I was in the middle of something that I had no control over and, unlike the incident in college, I didn't do anything wrong, but still they're not letting me play ball, taking the game away from me. So time was moving slow. The trial was taking place in Texas. I know now how the system works because I'm older, but back then I didn't know. But I'm sure the lawyer for the Spurs and the judge probably played golf together. I do remember the ABA commissioner Mike Storen getting involved and trying to help the Squires get me back, but the owner had already sold the team to someone else. Drossos had agreed to give me back to the Squires in return for the $225,000 plus interest and whatever legal fees he had to pay plus George Carter, but those businessmen in Virginia, who'd bought the team from Foreman, didn't want to make the deal. So Drossos filed a suit to finalize the deal. As I joked later in life: when Drossos went to work, we all know what happens. So even though it probably took longer than a month it was a done deal, the Spurs ended up winning the case, the Squires kept the money, and I became a San Antonio Spur.

That was my first real understanding of the business aspect of basketball, which until then I didn't take too seriously. Coming from the Continental League, I was just happy to be hoopin'. But that's when my mind opened up. San Antonio felt that I could help its franchise, so it put up the money to buy my contract. But I didn't have any feelings toward it. To me, I was just on another team. I had feelings about leaving Fatty Taylor and all of those guys. But remember I was just 21. I wasn't married. No kids. I was still hanging out at Norfolk State, I was at Hampton Institute, at Richmond

Coliseum, all them places. Basically, to a degree, still a college student. At that time I'm driving a nice car, and all of them on those campuses were hungry, so I used to go over there to the cafeteria and say "Who wanna eat?" They were all-Black colleges basically, so I knew how it was, and I was having fun. Then I get traded to San Antonio and ain't one black college there and I don't know anything about San Antonio except the Alamo. And when I got there, they didn't even have an R&B music station. And once they got it, it only came on one station at a certain time of day. That's what I was dealing with. And that's after I came from Virginia by way of Detroit, the Black music capital of the world at that time. So early on, yeah, I missed the hell outta Virginia from a social aspect—until I started hoopin.' And then I fell in love with San Antone.

In May of that same year in 1974, the Phoenix Suns actually drafted me in the third round of the NBA draft with the 40th pick overall. But I wanted to stay where I was, even though I was being coached by Tom Nissalke. He was all about discipline. That wasn't fun for me, and I'm not sure ownership was happy with our style of play under him. He used to coach the Dallas Chaparrals in the ABA before they moved and became the Spurs and he coached the Sonics in Seattle in the NBA before he came back to be the Spurs coach. In the beginning of the 1974–75 season, they fired him, and he ended up coaching the Utah Stars and Moses Malone. The Spurs put in Bob Bass to replace Nissalke.

Now keep in mind: at the time I got to the Spurs—as much as it was different than it was in Virginia—it was sort of still the same. I came to the Spurs midway through the organization's first season as a franchise. So that's not that much different than me coming to the Squires at midseason of my first season as a pro. We're both trying to figure things out. But Bass made the game fun again. And he became one of my favorite people in San Antonio. Bass was the one who had the vision to say, "Ice, I'm putting you at guard." Changed my career.

I fought it because in my mind I'd always been a forward, played there. Plus, I was 21 years old, so what did I know? But Bass was like, "Well I don't really give a damn what you wanna play." He was one of those kinda brothas. But literally from the first game, my career changed. Everything became so easy. Took me to another level right away. Opened up the game. I could do everything. I'd played against a lot of smaller guards coming up, so I always had an advantage. I'm 6'6", 6'7" battling against guys 6'1" so I knew how they would try to stop me. They would either try to steal the ball while I was dribbling or block it on my shot every time I tried to come up. So I knew. But my preparation made it easy when Bass switched me to a guard. I already knew how to get low to stop them from trying to steal the ball. Once I stood back up to shoot, they were still low because they were smaller. My goal was to simply keep them from taking the ball because after that there was nothing they could do with me. Bass putting me at the two was genius. Now the Spurs could build a franchise around me. At the forward spot, you couldn't.

I was so explosive at the guard position. And I didn't have to shoot a lot to get my numbers. That meant everyone else could be involved. Think about the guys who had to shoot a lot to get 30 or 40 points. James Harden averaged 36, wasn't getting everyone else involved. Before Michael Jordan started winning championships, he could have averaged 40, but he realized he could average 30 and be more efficient by letting Scottie Pippen and John Paxson and Horace Grant do their things. Once those guys started getting their 15 points a game, Jordan's 30 really meant something. And Jordan would take the last shots. Coach Bass was the same way with me. The game just got easier for me.

Still, James Silas was the man in San Antonio my first two or three years with the Spurs. He was averaging 23 points a game, and I averaged around 21. Then he got hurt. Then my average, well, it became what it became. Then, I was The Man. And I ain't ever look at myself as a franchise guy. I didn't even know what a franchise guy was. But at that time, it was me.

Early on in my time in San Antonio, I was playing house with Joyce. And right around the same time, Drossos was about to sign my new contract with the Spurs. He said to me, "GG, why you running around her playing house? You got that beautiful girl. Why don't you just get married and make it real?"

And at the time, Joyce was pregnant with Gee, our first child. When Drossos asked me that, I'd never thought about it. I was only 24. But once he asked, it hit me. Right after that we went to the courthouse and got married. 7/7/76. We married on the same day as Walter Payton and Connie Payton got married. Ain't that something? What I didn't know then was that Joyce and I were not living the way you are supposed to live. *We're having fun, we're together, we don't have to get married.* That's what I was saying to myself. And no matter what I said, I wasn't living right. But I trusted Drossos. He was one of those older men in my life and he wanted my life to be whole. Beyond just basketball. And he didn't tell me to get married; all he did was ask, "Why don't you?" Made me ask myself the same thing. He made me think about the direction of my life.

That was a very touching time for me. It was the best thing that ever happened to me. We didn't do anything big or lavish. My mom, my sister, Joyce's mom all came to the courthouse in San Antonio. We just let them read us the vows and we kissed, went back home, and just kept doing what we were doing. But then we're legal. We're official. We're right. I really honored our relationship from the very beginning, and this day for who we were. And as I realized later, I also honored the God who created our relationship because that's what He wanted.

* * *

The ABA was fun and crazy. When I was scoring in bunches and coming to Indianapolis to play the Indiana Pacers, some fast-food joint had this promotion where if they held me under 30 points, everybody would get a free chicken or a hamburger. On the public-address system, they kept mentioning the promotion. They were realy serious. They were advertising it, and we saw it on our way into the arena. Well, I got 55 on them that night. And as I walked off the court after the game, I sorta loudly said to the people in the crowd and to the Pacers, "Ain't nobody eating on Ice."

Though the Pacers kept going, the Memphis Sounds, San Diego Sails, Utah Stars, and Virginia Squires all folded, and the teams that were left were just playing each other over and over again. That was the season of the famous All-Star Game, the one where we as All-Stars played against the Denver Nuggets team in Denver. San Antonio Spurs owner

Angelo Drossos and Nuggets general manager Carl Scheer don't get enough credit for what they did that year in creating the first real All-Star Weekend. Glen Campbell performed at halftime of the game, and we had the first ever slam dunk contest. For us that was a beautiful weekend. It was created by two gentlemen who had a vision. Unfortunately, they are no longer around to appreciate what their actual vision has become.

But that dunk contest? C'mon. I wasn't no dunker. I shouldn't have even been in that. *Going against Dr. J? David Thompson, Larry Kenon, Artis Gilmore?* All of those guys dunk better than I did. It wasn't like I couldn't dunk, but that wasn't my forte. There was a guy who played with us on the Spurs named Henry Ward. I kept saying, "You all need to get Henry to do this." Because he dunked so easy. He'd actually jump up to the rim on two feet and throw the ball down where it never hit the rim and barely moved the net. Like the ball would come straight down, like it was shot from the ceiling. But his name wasn't big, and they were all about name recognition. And I did it because it was something to do. Plus we were on stage. It was part of the whole thing, but I went in knowing that I wasn't gonna win. I couldn't outdunk Doc, Kenon, or Thompson. Gilmore and I were the two big stiffs. And nothing against ol' Gilmore, but he ain't ever have creativity. (I kid you,

Artis.) So we were thankful to be a part of history, to be in the first dunk contest, but other than that, I knew I didn't have a chance.

In the end it ended up being only four teams that merged into the NBA from the ABA when it folded—the Nuggets, Pacers, New York Nets, and Spurs. The rest of the players were going to be dispersed, so NBA teams could pick them up, or any of the ABA teams, who merged and had roster openings, could pick them up. The merger was the best thing to happen to us as far as franchises even as a lot of the players got lost. I was fortunate. I was with a franchise that was solid, one the NBA felt could hold up. Drossos and Scheer knew the business. They were smart, and Drossos ended up getting Executive of the Year once we got into the NBA. And then they had me. And at that time, I guess I was a franchise guy because I was one of the guys who was part of the organization having stability.

Plus everyone wanted to be an NBA player anyway. It was still considered the best basketball. They had a television package, so the public knew who NBA players were. You very seldom saw us in the ABA on TV. We were a word-of-mouth league. Doc was the only one who was pretty much well-known from the ABA. I used to call him "Mr. ABA" because he was all you really heard about. And deservedly so. But to me I always felt we had some players coming from the ABA who deserved some opportunities to be in the NBA, which at the time we were calling "The Big League." And we ABA players, who got the chance to play in the Big League, gave the NBA the foundation it needed at that time.

We all know right now the NBA is the ABA. Whether everybody wants to say it or not, that's a different story. But the game is being played now the same way it was when we were playing with that red, white, and blue ball. Matter of fact: it's at that point now where they're doing everything that the ABA did *but* play with that red, white, and blue ball. Scheer and Drossos don't get any credit for what they created with the All-Star extravaganza that the NBA has as their All-Star Weekends now. They created that. The NBA didn't have that; it just had an All-Star Game on Sunday. These guys brought the entertainment, the ABA artistry, and history—everything the NBA is doing now. The whole ball movement, high scoring, using our three-point line. Are they going to give the ABA that credit? I doubt it very seriously. It would be nice to recognize that the ABA was a big part of what the NBA has grown to become and to sell that part of the game's history, but is that going to happen? Naw. It makes you wonder why.

Who's holding that narrative?

We were fighting for former ABA players to get a pension the same way we've been fighting to get our ABA stats officially included onto our NBA careers. I got 26,595 points in both leagues. They only count 20,708. So you go from me being in a top 20 all-time scoring leader in basketball history to me being down to 45th. So if you play that narrative, a lot of these guys are going to have more points than I did. Doc's the same way. With his ABA numbers, he has more than 30,000 points. Ain't but eight players ever scored 30,000 in the game, but Doc's at No. 75 on that all-time scoring list. It's a shame to not be able to utilize that part of our careers that has made the NBA what it really is today.

It's a great public conversation to have. I was on the advisory board of the Dropping Dimes Foundation for getting a pension for the former ABA guys who never got to play in the NBA. I'm glad they finally recognized those guys in that way. To see the NBA grow like it has globally, it would be nice for the ABA guys to financially hear a thank you. It's a drop in the bucket for a multi-billion dollar corporation, but it's a life-altering amount for a guy who played way back then to be able to use a pension or something just so they can hold their heads up high. To some of these guys, that pension money they're going to get is generational money. It's owed to them. Doc and I talk about it all of the time: how important it is to recognize these guys while they're still here. It's only like 115 or 120 of us left. And I played against a lot of those guys. But I was able to go on and have an NBA career; a lot of those guys weren't. That left a lot of players just out there with no basketball home. Even though they had a dispersal draft, many didn't make it, and some of those guys had been in the ABA the whole time the league was in existence. It's only fair that they get some restitution.

And the NBA needed that injection from the ABA. The '70s and '80s were some tight times, too. That was pretty much what they called the alcohol and drug-infested times. But the game grew. And then Magic and Bird came. Now they all say they feel Magic and Bird are the ones who turned it around, but I think the ABA was the foundation of that. Just look at the NBA All-Star team after the merger. See how many of those ABA players are on there. Bob Costas, who used to announce ABA games, even later noted at a recent ABA reunion that in the first year after the merger, 1976–77, 10 of the 24 players in that year's NBA All-Star Game had played in the ABA; half of the 10 starters in that year's NBA Finals between the Philadelphia 76ers and Portland Trail Blazers had played in the ABA. That shows how we brought in guys who helped rebuild their foundation. People can say what they want to say, but the proof is right there. And I'm not taking anything away from Magic or Bird and them, but they came *after* us. I'm not gonna sit up here and say we saved the NBA, but it needed something to bring it back to life. And we ABA players were the Vitamin D.

CHAPTER EIGHT

NIKE

All that dirt you put on it is going to blow away.

When I go to the campus at Nike—and I say this with a lot of confidence—I ain't up nowhere. There's no building for me, nothing like that. And I don't care. That's theirs. Because when you are talking about the Swoosh, I know the role I played. That's why I've never gone anywhere else because I appreciate the relationship. That's why former business affairs director of brand marketing for Nike Mark Thomashow, who I worked with closely for more than 30 years, is so important. I love being a part of a foundation. I'm satisfied with my relationship with Nike, satisfied with the money I made. They paid me well. Plus, it's satisfying for me to have that relationship and foundation with them. I have family, and my family knows the history.

I never approached them about having my own shoe. That was never important to me. I had a shoe, though, that Nike had made for me that had "ICE" on the back. A Blazer. And I played in them. So I did have a shoe (with my name on it), but nothing Nike specifically promoted. But I was probably their first signature ballplayer in basketball. Whether I get credit for it or not. I was a part of when Phil Knight was trying to take the company to the next level. I was with Knight when he was trying to put it together to make it work. It went from Knight selling shoes from his trunk to Ice to Michael Jordan to Bo Jackson. Can't forget him. Those to me are the two biggest names in Nike's history. And in the end, Nike has grown to almost a trillion-dollar company now. And I know basketball-wise, I am a part of that foundation.

My first couple of years as a pro, I played in Adidas. I wore those Pro Models like everyone else. Sometimes you could catch me playing in Chuck Taylors, sometimes in Pumas. It wasn't really about what was on my feet back then; it was about what was happening when that ball was in my hands. Nike was brand new and young when I signed with the company. They had Sidney Wicks and Geoff Petrie before I came there, but there weren't many players who wore them. We were all part of what I like to call "the ground floor." And the brand would not be what it is today if you didn't have the people on the ground floor there to build that foundation for the company to grow. And I kid Knight and them all the time about that.

We used to have what they called "The Pro Club." It was a group of us Nike basketball players that they used to take on trips to Hawaii and Sun Valley in Idaho in the offseason. We'd take our whole families. We'd take maids, babysitters, and anyone else we wanted to bring. It was unbelievable. Artis Gilmore was there. Spencer Haywood. Phil Chenier.

Rudy T. Austin Carr. All of the guys. I used to play tennis while all of the other guys played golf. It was like a vacation. We used to have the times of our lives. Everything and anything we wanted. The only thing Nike asked was that we not get anything out of the gift shops. They put us up in these beautiful hotels and resorts, but, of course, guys started getting things out of the gift shops. Messed our whole set-up up. Nike's giving us all of the clothes and shoes and things we want, we eating for free, we playing golf for free. *Everything is taken care of, and some guys do the opposite of what they ask you not to do?* After that Nike stopped doing it. There's always something where somebody ruins something for everybody. I think after that, though, Nike did start something similar back up again with a different group of players and coaches.

I wasn't the first guy at Nike to wear its basketball shoe, but me wearing the shoe at the time that I did and being the recognized player that I was helped make the brand more popular. I know that for a fact. I was in Virginia and then San Antonio, two of the smallest markets on the national level you could be in at that time. Yet, I was one of the ones they pushed out, which worked great for me but also really well for the brand. That is why I look at Nike as a partnership more than anything else. And probably pretty much why I'm still Nike through and through, even though I don't even have a contract with them. I have something better: I have a 45-year relationship.

Still, I look around sometimes and laugh to myself: *How all these brothas get these jobs at Nike, and I'm one of the ones who helped start Nike and I can't get a job from them*? Even though there are probably only a few former ballplayers who actually work for Nike, my point is that I was not thinking as a young man when I signed with Nike. I didn't really need the money because I was already making money. What I should've done was sign for shares of stock, but we didn't know anything about stocks. My agents and none of them knew about stocks. It was early, and Nike was still growing. I could have easily signed for that, but we didn't have that vision. Now my man, Knight, is sitting around with so much money he doesn't know what to do with himself.

I give Nike all of the credit in the world for inventing the ICEMAN poster. Did I see it becoming such an iconic thing? Heck, naw! Ain't no way. After we shot it, I didn't take it any further than that. Once the photo shoot was over, that was it for me. I didn't deal with it anymore until the poster came out. And then when it came out, people just kept getting it. They came up to me in the streets, everywhere I went, saying "Hey, man, I got that poster." They even had an ICEMAN poster night in Golden State! *In Golden State*. I was on the opposing team! That was amazing to me. That's when I was like, *Okay, this poster is on its way.* It became worldwide.

We shot that poster in an icehouse in Seattle in either 1977 or in 1978. And I can't remember how long it was after we shot it that Nike began selling it. All I thought about while shooting that poster though was getting off that ice. I was freezing. My butt was cold as I don't know what. It was real ice. I came there, and they built that throne as I was sitting there waiting. The poster during the shoot was secondary to me. If you really look at the poster of me sitting down, you can see the plastic they put on the ice to keep my sweatsuit from getting wet. And during the whole time I kept saying, "Hey, hey man, I need a break." I had to thaw out, which is kinda funny looking back. I was trying to get the feeling back in my butt and my legs. They took hundreds of pictures, different poses. So my biggest joy was getting off that ice and getting up out of there. But it turned out to be special. People still talk about it today, and I still sign those posters today more than 40 years later. The San Antonio Spurs front office still sends out smaller versions of it.

I signed a poster for Dick Gregory's son, Christian, and he likes to tell the story about the time we had with his father in a Kevin Durant Nike commercial. For us within the African American community, Dick Gregory was an icon. He stood for something, he stood for human rights, he stood for equality. He never asked anyone for anything. All he asked was for people to be fair, and then we can make our own way. He was one of the powerful voices we had in the 1960s and 1970s. He was an activist, a well-known author, and also a conspiracy theory guy. He always researched things himself, saw things his own way from the research he did, and was able to digest that information and put them in words. I was in awe of him, had a lot of respect for him.

He was also a famous comedian. He used to be on Dick Cavett's show and at the Playboy Clubs with Hugh Hefner. He was up there with the Redd Foxx's and the Moms Mabley's. But unlike some of them, Mr. Gregory used his comedy as commentary. He became famous for his approach to food and diet for Black people because he felt many Black people's lives were being lost due to our heath, and a lot of our health issues came from our diets and the food we were eating. His approach to food and diet was almost spiritual. It made many of us forget he was a comedian because we began looking at him as almost a spiritual kind of leader because of how he was trying to save so many of us through what we were doing to our bodies. So, for me, having Dick Gregory in Nike commercials was a big deal.

Anyhow, we were in Austin, Texas. Charles Oakley was in the commercial, so he was there, too. Mr. Gregory had a 1,000-acre farm in Plymouth, Massachusetts. So while they're telling me about life on their farm, I was telling them about my 30-acre ranch and how I always saw rattlesnakes. It scared Dick Gregory because he can't deal with even the thought of snakes. He said, "We gonna stop calling you 'The Iceman' and call you 'The Snakeman.'" But what was really funny was him saying to me: "George, can you believe this? Dick Gregory doing a Nike commercial for these White folks!"

That was a great time, and Christian loved that poster. "When executed perfectly, art can dictate motion," he said. He told me when he was eight years old he didn't know who I was because he didn't watch sports. But then he was at a sporting goods store in that same town they lived in and saw the poster hanging up. He said seeing this Black man on a throne of ice, palming two metallic silver basketballs was the coolest thing he'd ever seen in his life. The Gregory farm back then was a big deal. Celebrities would come there. Michael Jackson, Eddie Murphy. Politicians. Icons. Christian saw all of these people come to his house, and the only poster he ever had on his wall as a kid—the only one—was the ICEMAN poster. And he says it wasn't until four-to-five years later that he even found out who I was. For him that poster represented a form of activism. He told me, "George, people always think of activism as people with signs and civil rights voices, but most of us are activated by seeing something powerful and being moved by it." To the son of an iconic, legendary activist, my poster hanging on his wall was his activism.

Rick Mahorn talked about how he still has the poster hanging on his wall in his home. I heard Chris Paul talk about growing up with the poster and how it was his father's favorite because I was his father's favorite player. Bobby Portis of the Milwaukee Bucks a few years ago posted a photo of Giannis Antetokounmpo replacing me in the poster. Same pose and everything with the words "Greek Freak" instead of "Iceman." Stacy Wall, who's the guy who wrote and helped create a lot of the Nike commercials I was in, hand painted the special Spanish version of the poster with the "El HOMBRE DE HIELO" at the bottom. Back in 2012, when Knight gave his Hall of Fame speech for his induction into the Naismith Basketball Hall of Fame, he talked about my poster. And things like that mean something to me because it shows the impact that single poster had on people. And I still can't explain why.

The poster during those times in the '70s was the one of Farrah Fawcett. All they talked about was Fawcett's poster. Then, you started hearing them say, "Man, I had Farrah Fawcett *and* the Iceman posters on my wall." And, man, that humbled me. The whole poster phenomenon to me grew out of humility. That's how I really feel. Humbled that someone would ask about putting me on a poster, so I'm not bragging about it or anything. And when you appreciate things in life they seem to grow at a different pace. That's how it was with the poster.

CHAPTER NINE

TEAMMATES

I don't know if anyone else will tell them thanks, but I will.

The ABA was almost considered, especially to the Red Auerbachs and most of the general managers and people around the NBA, a league of a bunch of guys who couldn't play, who couldn't make it in the NBA. To them, we were like a farm team before farm teams were created. The NBA was the established league, it was known worldwide. That was the league to be in. So in '76 when we merged, it just changed. Man, I was excited to be on that stage, to say that I was not an ABA guy anymore but an NBA guy. And I never thought I wasn't ready, never thought like I didn't belong. All I wanted to do was be consistent. Anybody can have a couple of good games, but I wanted to show that I could be effective in the league. I tried to progressively show people in the league and NBA fans that I was for real and that I could play well no matter who was guarding me. I'm not saying that I was better than anyone else. I never took that attitude, but at the same time, I didn't feel that anyone even in the NBA could guard me.

I did my research and realized usually the leading scorers in the league during that era and even leading up to that era were on teams at the bottom. Nate Archibald with the

Kansas City Kings, Pete Maravich with the New Orleans Jazz, Elvin Hayes with the San Diego Rockets. So it was a great accomplishment to me that I won my scoring title, and we still won the division. I could score, and we could still make the playoffs, still be recognized—even in only our second season—as one of the better teams in the NBA. Kareem Abdul-Jabbar is the first one I can remember who led the league in scoring and ended up winning the championship. That was the year Oscar Robertson got there with him for the Milwaukee Bucks in 1971. Even Wilt Chamberlain last won the scoring title in 1966, but he didn't win his first championship until the year *after* that. Basically, scorers in the NBA didn't get associated with winning. I wanted to change that.

I was excited. To play against the Boston Celtics, man, and *John Havlicek*. He was Mr. Basketball during that period, running off those picks, dribbling one or two times before he shot that jumper. The Celtics set up plays for him, and you had to follow him while he was weaving and swerving and never stopping and getting that rock and shooting it in your face. He'd get 17, 18 points on you easy. Sometimes in the first half. That was exciting to me. I wish he was still alive so that I could ask him if it was exciting for him to play against me. For me as a student of the game and as someone who loved to be on the floor with those guys after all of those years in the ABA, it just made me feel that I'd made it. I got to play against some of the greatest of all time. Walt Frazier. I remember I played against him once. He was with the Cleveland Cavaliers at the time, and it was after his New York Knicks days. He told me, "You know, Ice, right now, you The Man."

I said, "I'm the what?" Now I heard what he said, but it was coming from him, so it didn't register with me. I couldn't believe he was saying that *to me*. I was still a student in the game, still learning, still respecting the guys who I watched all of my basketball life. And for Frazier to say that *to me*? And it was a moment that was just between us. He probably doesn't even remember it if you asked him. But it meant so much to me. Very similar to what Jerry West said to me. Those things I will never forget.

Our first year in the NBA, we, the San Antonio Spurs, led the NBA in scoring. From 1978 to 1980, we averaged 118 points per game. Just to put that in perspective, in 2021–22 the Minnesota Timberwolves and Memphis Grizzlies led the NBA in scoring with 116. Which all leads back to Jimmy Silas. The NBA never really got a chance to see Silas play. He was their first franchise guy, one of the most underrated 6'1" or 6'2" guards in NBA history. He got hurt first in the first game of our last playoff series in the ABA. I was getting a lot of the attention, but he was the one who was first-team

All-ABA before we came to the NBA, not me. He was our leader, "the Man" of the franchise, and I followed him, followed his lead. I was his understudy—same as with Dr. J on the Virginia Squires—watching how he did it and he brought it every night. I'm the one who told our coach, Bob Bass, to "give the ball to Jimmy Si" late in the games because "he'll get it done." That's the way our team was built when we merged. Then Doug Moe came over from the Denver Nuggets to be our head coach, and in the preseason going into our first NBA season, Silas hurt his knee and he was never really the same. And my role changed.

* * *

I was missing Fatty Taylor. I've always believed he was just a born leader. Just his approach to the game was one aspect of it. Then just his personality and outlook on life. He was a motivator. When I left Virginia, I didn't really have anyone close to me anymore. That's because of how I came into the league. I came in raw. And Fatty put me under his wing. But who became Fatty to me in San Antonio was a guy by the name of Dennis "Mo" Layton. Mo reminded me of Fatty. He was a little older, had played for a few teams, but he was that kind of guy who'd be like, "Hey man, you don't know how good you are."

I'd just say to him the same thing I said to Fatty, "Well, I ain't ever tried to figure out how good I am."

I knew what I could do, but I never looked or approached the game as a battle. Not even a battle within myself. But Mo challenged me, especially on the defensive end. He'd say to me, "Man, you gonna let that dude score on you? C'mon, Ice." He did that all season. I'd end up blocking three or four shots a game, and Mo'd be like, "See, see, see." And that ended up being the season I had 110 blocked shots. So I've always credited him for my defensive improvement.

In our second year in the NBA, I led the league in scoring. I wasn't trying to be a franchise player or the face of the San Antonio Spurs. I was just consistent. I wasn't one for the attention and I always gave back to my guys, my teammates, because I couldn't do what I was doing without them. But on that court, I was still gonna do me. I was bred to play. But I had some brothas around me. I attribute much of my success to Fatty because he helped me understand my own ability.

But playing alongside Jimmy Silas for those few years gave me an understanding about leadership. Even though Si and I came into the ABA the same year, he was three years older than I was. And he was drafted by the Spurs so he was with them a year before I was traded there. So I took a back seat. It wasn't like we were best of friends, but we were teammates and we respected one another. We spent time together. If there's no more time left, we're down one, and he's shooting two free throws, I knew I could walk to the locker room because I knew he wasn't going to miss. I would tell the coaches at the end of games, "Put the ball in his hands."

Si was that effective. He would get fouled because those little guards would try to bang against him, but he was strong, had that good back-to-the-basket bump game, and got great separation to shoot that jumper. All of those little guards didn't fear him, but they respected his ability to put the ball in the hole or get free throws. Especially when games were on the line. He was clutch down the stretch. That's how he got those nicknames, "Captain Late" and "The Late Mr. Si." He was special in that way. That's why when he got hurt it was so unfortunate. A lot of the guys who played against him will say the same thing. But we know that's how the game is. You're always one play from not playing again, not being able to play the way you once did, or losing your confidence after you come back. A lot of things can happen. And Si was never the same guy after his injuries, even though he still had some good seasons. The Spurs ended up trading him. It was the season after we lost to Moses Malone and the Houston Rockets in the conference semis.

Si was the first teammate of mine, where I was able to watch and see how the game functions when you are not producing the way the team feels it needs you to be in order to keep the product going. When that happens, they move you and bring somebody else in. When guys like Si and other players, who were once franchise players, get hurt or aren't the same, they move you. And usually after that, you get moved around. Si was fortunate; he only had to deal with that once.

One thing I do love, though, is that Silas was the first retired number of the Spurs organization. They did look out and they did show him that love. Now I want them to show that same kinda love to Larry Kenon. K averaged a double-double. First ever for the franchise and no one else has averaged a double-double except David Robinson and Tim Duncan, and both of their numbers are in the rafters. One of the local San Antonio news guys, Don Harris, and I talk about it all of the time: when is the franchise going to respect him in that way? K played for the Spurs five years. Was one of the greatest Spurs. When is that going to be recognized? This is what I hope for before he's gone.

K and I were pretty close. And one thing: he loved the game. K came from Birmingham, Alabama. He'd won a title with Dr. J in the ABA playing with the New York Nets before he came to San Antonio. K could run, score, rebound. He knew how to play and he wanted to win. I keep saying that we had enough to win a championship, and he was a big part of me believing that. I knew we could win with K. I knew we could win with Mike Mitchell. Once we got Artis Gilmore, our chances of winning a championship went up even higher. And Mitchell is another one who I feel gets overlooked. He's another lost jewel. All you have to do is go back and research to see how dominant he was. Go talk to the guys he played against back in that era. Mitchell and I grew to be pretty close, too. He had one of the best turn-around bank shots in the game of basketball in that era. And was consistent. He averaged 20 points a game for his career. Always shot around 50 percent.

Then there was Mike Gale. Man could guard anybody. He reminded me of a bigger Fatty. He would *guard* people, was always up in them. He had an ol' funny-looking shot, but he could make it. He could pass the ball and run a team. He was a bad boy. Out of Elizabeth City. He was a Jersey dude.

Another guy was Johnny Moore. He and I are one of the few tandems in NBA history who together as teammates won the assist and scoring title in the same season. We did it eight years later in the 1981–82 season. Moore passed the ball, guarded people, and got better over the years because he couldn't shoot at first. I always used to mess with him, I'd be like, "Johnny, look here: you keep letting these guys double-team me, you keep letting your man come over here and double-team me, and when I pass you the ball and you don't shoot, you don't make that jumper, I'm a shoot on both of them."

He'd always say, "I'm a make it, Ice. Just throw it to me. Keep throwing it to me. I'm a make those shots." And he did. In one game against the Denver Nuggets, Doug Moe was back there coaching them and he double-teamed me the whole game, and I kept dropping the ball off to Moore, and he got 30 points. And he afterward was like, "I told you, Ice. I told you I'll hit those shots."

And once we got Gilmore in San Antonio, I felt he was the missing piece to take us to the next level. He was the biggest, strongest guy in basketball at that time. His percentage shooting-wise was close to 60 percent. He blocked shots. He and I were close. We're still close. We both came over from the ABA, but he landed with the Chicago Bulls and played there for six years before the Spurs made a move to get him. Even though he'd won a title in the ABA in '75 with the Kentucky Colonels and was the Finals MVP, not winning a championship with Gilmore in the NBA with the Spurs was disappointing for me, mostly because of how I feel about him. But having him on the Spurs as a teammate gave us the confidence to feel that we could win one. Especially having to face the Los Angeles Lakers. In Gilmore we had someone who was going to give Kareem Abdul-Jabbar some pushback. Because you're not going to stop Jabbar, but we had someone to give him some resistance.

We had a crew we called "the Bruise Brothers." They were a part of the team on our team. Mark Olberding, Paul Griffin, Coby Dietrick, George Johnson. When I needed somebody to get somebody off me, they were the brothas I'd call on. Olberding was the one. He came outta Minnesota, real young, a tough son of a gun. "Ding-Ding" was a banger. So when a guy was guarding me real hard, I'd say, "Hey Ding-Ding, get him off me, man."

And Ding-Ding would say, "Okay, Ice, bring him over here." Like he was a mob enforcer or something. So I'd fake right, and Ding was to the left, and then I'd cut real hard to the left, and Ding would be there, waiting on him. They never saw it coming. And I ended up shooting wide-open jumpers.

Griffin was the same. Dietrick was the same. He used to talk to me during games, "Ice do this, Ice do that." Beautiful, beautiful young man. Deitrick was announcing games for the Spurs for a while after we retired and was good at it. But like anything else, when ownership changed, then there's personnel change. I think he got caught up in that. Great teammate. All of those guys had knowledge of the game. I played with Allan Bristow, who went on to become a coach and general manager in the league. Special guys.

Then there's Gene Banks. Now there's a special guy. I didn't know anything about him until he came to San Antonio. I didn't know the whole Duke thing and him being the ACC Rookie of the Year of that team that went to the NCAA Championship Game his freshman year. And how big of a deal that was. His personality, his love for the game, his hustle, that's what made him. He wasn't a great shooter, wasn't a great rebounder, but he was a great utility guy. He was small for his position in them days. He was around 6'7", but he was playing the four, power forward. But he was smart, knew how to keep the ball alive, set good picks, motivate, and was a great locker room guy. Always had great stories. Banks was that guy who played a big role when we played the Lakers in those battles. With his size—because he was solid, around 215 to 220 pounds—and his love for the game and the fact that he stayed active on the court, he could and would guard anybody. He didn't care. And he was always fun to be around. Over the years I probably have stayed in closer touch with him than any of my teammates with the exception of Gilmore. Banks and I played five years together. The relationships with them has never been one-sided with me. Whenever we see each other, we see each other with admiration. I took the game to a level that none of them was able to, but I know none of what I was able to achieve would have ever been reached without them. And I've always tried to make sure that they know that. They've always felt a part of my life; it's more than just someone I played ball with. I've never separated myself from them.

They mean a lot to me because I've always felt the game is designed to be played one way: as a team. Now the goal is to win, but everybody don't. More actually don't than do. So what goes into that team concept? It's more than just passing each other the ball and someone putting the ball in the hole. It's about getting to know one another. All of these guys, my teammates, helped make me who I became. I credit those guys for being a part of all the success I had on that court. They all deserve a lot more attention than they get. We didn't win it all, but we won consistently. Year after year after year. Division titles, playing in the conference finals. I got—still get—a lot of the attention and credit, but the reality is it ain't mine. A lot of my teammates are a big part of not only my success and my career, but also the success of the Spurs organization. I have a lot to be thankful for—especially the relationships I have with those brothers.

Along with Gilmore and Banks, K proved to be a good friend. Beyond just a teammate, especially when I was struggling, dealing with my issues. He'd say, "Hey G, just live." (He called me "G," never called me "Ice.") He had his own way of telling me that so that I knew what he meant. That's another of those things I'll never forget. I'll always remember how important that was to me at that time in my life. I tell him to this day how much I appreciate him for encouraging me. He may call on occasion to ask me for something.

"Hey man, you know I don't like calling asking anybody for anything, but..."

And I always say, "K, you can ask me for anything because you were there for me when I really needed to hear an encouraging word." That's how important he was as a teammate, and I ain't talking about ball. I'm talking off the court about that brotherhood you always hear us ballplayers talk about, I'm talking about life. That's the kind of respect and love brothers have over the years for one another. We go through things together, life things. And when a brotha needs an uplifting word, you'd be surprised where it comes from: one of your teammates. I wasn't expecting it. K reached out to me. "Hey, G, just live man." That's all he said, all he had to say.

* * *

April 9, 1978 was a Sunday. We're in New Orleans, playing the Jazz in the final game of the season. It was pretty hot, 85 degrees. But not that Texas hot that I was getting accustomed to after being in San Antone for five years so far. New Orleans had a little humidity with their heat. Our game was at the Superdome that afternoon, and we were staying at the New Orleans Hilton, a new hotel only like a year old about a mile from the Superdome. David Thompson and I were at the finish line for the scoring title. It had come down to the last game to see who was going to win it. I remember I had almost 2,200 points going into that game. Up until then I'd never scored more than 2,000 in a season. Thompson trailed me by two-tenths of a point going into that game. It was also the day of John Havlicek's final game in the Boston Garden. They had a ceremony and everything. His family was there, Red Auerbach spoke, the game was televised and everything. It was a big deal.

A reporter called my hotel room to tell me about what Thompson had done in Detroit against the Pistons because that game was not televised nationally. He told me I'd lost the scoring title. And I remember our coach, Doug Moe, being not too happy and saying the Pistons let Thompson go off for 73 points. Keep in mind he was Thompson's coach over in Denver before he came to us in San Antonio. So he knew what Thompson was capable of doing. And after being with me for two years, he knew what I was capable of doing, too. Moe wanted me to have that scoring title. I needed 59 points to get the title. All of my teammates and the coaches were like, "Let's help Ice get 59."

Fifty-nine points in forty-eight minutes. No three-pointers. The NBA hadn't adopted it into the league yet. People have to really respect you and appreciate you to help make that happen. It's not like I coulda done it by myself. I don't take that credit. Just them being willing to do that told me a lot about the kind of relationship I had with my guys. And that's why when anyone asks me what was my favorite season, I always go to that season and that game because it wasn't about me. I got the credit, but I didn't deserve it.

I started out 1-for-6. I said, "Forget it."

But the guys were like, "C'mon, Ice. C'mon! C'mon! C'mon!" I ain't ever heard so many "c'mons" in my life.

Moe called two timeouts the in first quarter. I'll never forget he yelled, "When I say nobody f------ shoots it, but Ice, I mean nobody shoots it but Ice!" Then I started rollin'. Had 20 by the end of the first quarter, had 33 in the second quarter, 53 at half. I was tired at halftime. Pete Maravich was technically in front of the points-per-game scoring that year before his knee injury, averaging 27.0, but even at that pace, had they allowed his 50 games and scoring average to stand, he still would have finished behind Thompson and me. But Pistol Pete was at that game in the Superdome cheering me on.

Thompson's contract was up, so the scoring title meant something to him. He said in his book that Maravich was under the same circumstances the season before when he scored 68 against the New York Knicks. I got to 59 pretty quick in the third quarter and ended the game with 63. Moe pulled me after that. Sat me down for the night. I took 49 shots and 20 free throws in 33 minutes. We lost the game by 20, 152–132. I was too tired to go out on Bourbon

Street afterward. It was the closest scoring race in the history of the NBA. Still is. Thompson said in his book: "It took me 16 years to break Wilt's [most points in a quarter] mark, but it only took Gervin seven hours to break mine."

The battle reached a mythical place because no recording of either game exists. Neither game was televised—probably because of all the attention that day being on Havlicek—and there's no video of them. The most historic scoring race in NBA history and there's no video evidence! But to me that's what makes it even more beautiful. It's left up to the people who were there and the stories that will be told. There's a great animated rendering someone did of the games. Of Thompson and me scoring, of Thompson and me talking, it's beautiful. Thompson said, "Who can go in to a game, need 59 points and get it...besides George Gervin?" That made my heart flutter. He said it with so much conviction. He believed it more than I did. And the beautiful thing is years later in 1996 we went into the Hall of Fame together.

CHAPTER TEN

GAMES

Your reflection becomes your learning.

Friday, May 18, 1979. Cap Centre, Washington, D.C. It was actually Landover, Maryland, but we all called it "D.C." Game Seven of the Eastern Conference Finals to go to the NBA Finals. The San Antonio Spurs against the Bullets, who were the defending champs. We had been up in the series three games to one, and only two other teams in the NBA had ever lost a series after being up 3–1. I was playing pretty good in the series, leading in scoring, averaging about 31 points a game. I shot 52 percent, was third in rebounding (38), second in blocks (10), led my team in steals (13). Everything was set up for us to go to the Finals.

Final score was 107–105. I scored 42 points, Bobby Dandridge for the Bullets scored 37—11 of them in the fourth quarter—and hit the winning jump shot from the baseline with fewer than 10 seconds left. Both of us went 16-of-31 shooting. But he got hot at the right time. I heard that his coach Dick Motta apparently told him to "go out there and win the damn game." On the last possession, we had a chance to send it into overtime. But Elvin Hayes blocked James Silas' shot, then Dandridge stole the ball from Larry

Kenon, and then the fans stormed the court. A headline in the Washington newspaper the next day was "Doing Things That Champions Do" and had a picture of me, Kenon, and Silas all looking up at Dandridge taking that last shot.

What's crazy is that for a series between us a year earlier, the lights went out. For 13 minutes the arena went dark in the third quarter. Right when we were going on a roll, took the lead. Killed our whole momentum. No one talks about it. Interesting history to that: Danny Ferry, the former Duke star and NBA player who ended up being a general manager in the NBA, was a kid at that game. His father Bob Ferry was the GM of the Bullets at the time. And Danny has said to me over the years, "Hey, George, I pulled the plug on the lights."

Now I know he says it in fun, but I believe him. At the time of the game, we were killing the Bullets. Silas felt like the game was stolen from us. Doug Moe was mad about the refereeing and said the refs needed to be "set before a firing squad." I went back and checked. In the final four minutes of the game after the lights went out, the refs called nine fouls—seven of them were on us. They went 11-for-15 from the foul line in the fourth quarter, and we went 3-for-4. And we're on the road. In their place. The defending champs. I remember saying to the reporters after the game: "Go talk to the winners. It's summertime for me. It's all over."

The playoff loss to the Bullets haunts me more than any other game in my basketball history simply because I believe it was my first real opportunity to win a championship. That game taught me something. Yeah I got 42 points, but I realized because of that game that sometimes 40 will get me good numbers, but 30 mighta got me the win. See everything was centered around me. I mean, that game taught me what it really takes to win. I learned about winning by losing. That was an education for me. Yeah, I got 42 in a Game Seven, I got 40-plus many a time, I got it in a situation that could have taken me to a NBA Finals. Now, I think if I should have been more of a facilitator than a scorer, more like Magic Johnson by making someone else better down the stretch, letting Kenon score a little bit more, taking the ball out of my own hands, putting it in his hands more to make them key on him, and making them play off him instead of playing off me. I've looked at that game all kind of ways. I'm proud of the way I played, I'm proud of that 42 I was able to get in that moment, but the nature of the game is to win, and I wanted to win.

I'm second-guessing everything when it comes to that game. *Should we have concentrated more on defense? Was it shot selection? Was it more about getting some other players involved? Was it our style of play? How could we have made sure to get another win?* We up 3–1! It's like a broken record inside my head. I keep thinking how the way we played got us there, but was it also the reason we weren't able to finish? Almost 45 years after the fact, I'm still trying to figure out how we didn't win.

That was probably the first time in my career that I got emotional. Because we let it get away. That made me realize how hard it is to get there, to just play to get to the Finals. We never got to that stage again. Never that close. We got to the Western Conference Finals against the Los Angeles Lakers in 1983, but we weren't up 3–1. But the Bullets had a championship squad. Great team. Hayes. Dandridge. Wes Unseld. Larry Wright was their point guard. Tom Henderson. He was also a good point guard. Greg Ballard. Kevin Grevey. They had three Hall of Famers on that team. They had six players averaging double figures in scoring for the series. But I still felt that we had a good enough team to win a championship regardless of what they had. I felt we could have beaten the Seattle SuperSonics in the NBA Finals if we'd gotten there. We had some guys who could play! I felt we could win it all, and that was our chance—and never got another one. Everybody doesn't get a shot, and I got a shot; that's the way I look at it. I was almost there. Never won a championship, never got to the Finals, never won an MVP. And today's media judges you by all that. So I know why I'm not included in some conversations because I never got there.

I question myself. And I ain't afraid to tell anybody: *Did I know what it took to win?* In that aspect of looking at the game of basketball, did I know at that time what it really took to win? LeBron James gets a lot of criticism because they say he doesn't take the last shot. My way of looking at it is, "If he's wide open and I'm double-teamed, I'm supposed to give one of my teammates the ball."

But people look at it as, "Well, Michael Jordan wouldn't have passed it, or Kobe Bryant wouldn't have passed the ball. They'd have shot over two people." Because of that James gets a knock. Gets hated on. I think James makes the right play. Especially in the middle part of his career, he made good situational decisions. It got him four championships. So when I dissect my only chance in that game to get to the Finals, I'm more critical of myself, thinking, *If I played like James, maybe if I'd just got 30 instead, involved everybody more, maybe we would've won.* Sometimes, in all sports, you just don't play smart. In that particular game, I don't think I played smart. And it cost me.

Eight months later back in Washington—my fault, Landover, Maryland—back on that exact same court where we'd lost to the Bullets, I can still see Tiny Archibald passing me the ball. I won the MVP of the All-Star Game. Larry Bird played with me, Dr. J was on my squad. Michael Ray Richardson, Hayes, and Moses Malone, too. That was the first All-Star Game of all of the ones I played in where I got aggressive. I didn't go out there saying I'm gonna win MVP, but I played aggressively. And I have no idea why. It made me wonder why I wasn't aggressive like that all of the time? I wasn't mad. No one pissed me off. My guess is that it just happened to be my time to shine. I even remember they called a travel on one of my breakaway dunks. Even during the game, Brent Musburger said he didn't see a travel. I still remember the referee who made the call. I've played in 12 All-Star Games—nine in the NBA, three in the ABA—and that really was the only one when I played assertive. All of the rest of them, I'd get 12, 13, and 15 points. But that game I don't know what it was—maybe it was connected to the loss I'd had in that same building eight months ago—but I came to play. And then obviously it's who I was playing with. On that All-Star team, there were nothing but winners. Maybe that was it.

The 1983 All-Star Game in Los Angeles was different. That was the one where Marvin Gaye sung the anthem. Pat Riley was the coach. He kept me out of the game. Now I've never done anything to Riley, but he never liked me. The way I was playing when I got in, the MVP of that game could have been me, but Dr. J got it. He played well, not taking anything from him, but Riley kept me out of the game. I played the fewest minutes—along with Kiki

Vandeweghe—of anyone on our team. It was almost like it was personal. Kareem Abdul-Jabbar wrote about it in his book; Magic and Michael Cooper have talked about it on podcasts.

But the next game after the All-Star break, we played the Lakers on a Tuesday. I did drop 40 on them that next game. I had the incentive to do something special in that game after that All-Star Game—and everybody knew it. Riley knew what kind of monster I was; he couldn't deny that. It was just a matter of whether or not I was going to be prepared to bring out the monster. I admit it; I took it personally. And I played that game against the Lakers as if it was personal. But Coop and Magic embellished the story, saying I was staring down Riley. I laugh at that because I've never been like that, but I do think what Riley did to me by sitting me in that All-Star Game was personal. He had his own reasons, whatever it was. Don't know what the reason is, don't care. But when someone has the power to make somebody else's life a little harder and they do it, it tells a lot about their character.

I had Riley again as the coach in my last All-Star Game in 1985, which was another one where I could have gotten MVP. That game it went to Ralph Sampson. I was rollin' in that one. Only missed two shots and ended up with 23 points. Sampson had 24 points. I'm not taking anything away from

Sampson—or Magic, who had like 15 assists in that game—and I'm not saying that I deserved the MVP of that game by no means. But I think I played well enough to get my second All-Star MVP trophy.

Now the regular season MVP is another thing. I *am* saying that in 1978–79 I could have won the MVP, and Bill Walton got it while only playing in 58 games. I maybe should have won, but they gave him MVP. I got 34 percent of the first-place votes, and he got 40 percent. It was after the Portland Trail Blazers won the championship, and they came out the next season rollin'. I think they won maybe 48 or 50 of the games Walton played in. And that was one of those seasons, where I not only led the league in scoring, but was also the Seagrams 7 Award for most efficient player. Injustice always follows us. We don't get what we deserve all of the time. But it's all about how you handle it.

I've been asked if I feel a certain way about it and I do. Because when you look at your career, you start naturally looking at the honors that you earned. Right or wrong, they too tell a story. In my case I was second in MVP voting two years in a row in 1977–78 and 1978–79. The second time was behind Moses Malone. But I can't let the way the narrative has been pushed impact the way I feel. It's no different in the NBA than it is in life. But if you look and do your own research, it tells its own story. But I think of Walton, too.

And he never have anything to do with it. I'm never going to try and lessen what he did or what he means to this game because I love Walton and I love his career. He was a bad boy, too. It was just that particular year he didn't happen to play many games. At the time it was the least amount of games any player had ever played and won an MVP. Karl Malone played fewer games when he won his 20 years later in 1999, but that was the lockout season, which was different. I have confidence in myself and am comfortable in who I am. But that doesn't stop me from feeling a particular way about it. But I know I'm in good company because Jerry West finished second in MVP voting four times and still never won one.

* * *

I played in this charity game during the summer. It was one of Magic Johnson's games. We used to play all of the time in the summer when Johnson became a young pro. We used to travel to all of the non-NBA cities and play and sell the places out. Back then was when Magic, Isiah Thomas, and Mark Aguirre really got to know me and used to come to my room, and we used to talk basketball all night. Talk to any three of those guys, and they'll tell you that's how we built the kind of affection for one another that we have because I was with them when they were young pros. And there was this one game in Magic's hometown of Lansing, Michigan, where this player, Kevin Loder, called me out. He was a rookie. During halftime of the game, I was sitting down, peeling an orange when Loder said, "Yeah man, I blocked Ice's finger roll!"

It was the summer so were just playing around out there, it ain't serious. But Loder kept saying it. "I'm gonna block Ice's finger roll."

I just looked up and said, "What's your name?" He said his name, and I went back to peeling my orange. I put 40 on that kid in the second half of that game. I think I ruined his career.

But I was comfortable in my skin. I already knew who I was. I never needed anybody to sell me. I already knew what I could do. What I always loved about the game is that other teams used to prepare whole defenses to stop me. And look at my shooting percentages as a guard: 53.6 percent, 54.1 percent, 52.8 percent, respectively, from 1970 to 1980; 50 percent again in 1981–82; and 51 percent for my NBA career. So I really have never cared what anyone had to say about me. They had to have a gameplan to stop this brotha because I was coming at 'em.

I played in a triple-overtime game against the Milwaukee Bucks in 1982. At that time it was the highest scoring game in NBA history. We won 171–166. I didn't have many 50-point games, but that game was one of them. What I remember most though was Mike Mitchell had 45 points in that game, and Brian Winters of the Bucks, who didn't start, still had 42 points. For me that game is not about the numbers I put up because I put up those kind of numbers more than once. But to put the spotlight on and expose a teammate, a guy like Winters, in a good way was great. People may not know him, but, man, that brother could shoot the lights out. And then to have two guys, teammates, score more than 40 apiece, that's unheard of.

No one talks about what Mitchell and I did in that game. It's the second most points scored by teammates who've both scored more than 40 points in a game in NBA history. We combined for 95 points. Only Kiki Vandeweghe and Alex English of the Denver Nuggets in a game against the Detroit Pistons two seasons later had more. They combined for 98. And that game also broke our record of the most total points scored in an NBA game. I feel they need to have a category just to recognize how rare it is. I'm recognized for my scoring, but Mitchell doesn't get recognized like he should. That's why I feel there should be something to distinguish those types of feats so that they are discussed more when they happen. In 2015 Klay Thompson and Steph Curry both had 50-point games in the same season, and I remember hearing at the time they were only the seventh teammates to do that, but how about two teammates almost doing it in the same game? People made a big deal out of Jamal Murray and Donovan Mitchell in that playoff game in the Bubble both scoring 50 points on each other. And I think that was the first time something like that happened in NBA history. So how rare must it be for two players on the same team to come close to reaching that 100-point mark? There's only been three games in NBA history where one teammate scored at least 50 points and another scored at least 40 points in the same game. It's a piece of history that more should know about.

The beauty of it was the shooting percentage of that game. Neither Mitchell nor I took a lot of shots. (The only time I really took a lot of shots was the game when I was chasing that scoring title against David Thompson. But that was the plan of that game, so that was different.) But this game against the Bucks, it was about efficiency. Mitchell had an unbelievable ability to score efficiently, too, and we never got in each other's way.

Our Western Conference Semifinal game against the Nuggets in 1983 was pretty special. It was Game One of the series. We put up 152 points! We had six players in double figures. Almost had four players in double digits in rebounding. We ended up winning the series in five games. But that game was one that stands out because this was after Thompson was gone, and the Nuggets still brought it. They still had

133 points. English had 26 points and 10 rebounds, and Vandeweghe had 22 points. Dan Issel had 28 points. They also had this Rob Williams outta Houston. Man, talk about a lost art. He could score, dribble, pass. I had 42 points with T.R. Dunn guarding me. And he's one of the players I talk about who always played good defense on me. He sits around now and laughs at me whenever I say that. He says, "Ice, you just bullshittin'."

And I always say, "I'm telling the truth. You, Michael Cooper, Dennis Johnson, Jamaal Wilkes, you all made me come to work."

Anyway, that series we were rollin'. That's when I really thought we had a chance to win it all. I averaged 28 points a game and shot better than 60 percent from the field that series. Johnny Moore averaged 27 points and 14 assists and shot over 60 percent. Gene Banks averaged 20 points a game and shot better than 50 percent. But those Los Angeles Lakers were a problem.

During that time in order to get out of the West, the Lakers were always there. And even though we only played them twice in the Western Conference Finals while I was there, I still considered Lakers–Spurs a rivalry. We could go into Lakerland during the regular season and tear a hole in their butts. Everybody couldn't do that. I won't say they feared us, but they knew we were there. They respected us enough to know that they had to stay on top of their game, or else we—not them—were going to the Finals. And they stayed on top of their game. And the Lakers weren't the only team who respected us. We were respected throughout the Western Conference as having a chance to win it. But after that 3–1 loss in 1979, the two times we had to get there, we had to go through them son of a guns. I hate that we never beat the Lakers in a series. It was a shame that we didn't. It's always made me wonder what adjustments could we have made?

I looked at the Lakers as great but also as a team we could bump off. I never conceded to them. But when you start talking about superteams, Lakers owner Jerry Buss knew where he needed to go and who he needed to get. He had the resources. He had the coaches. Had the general manager. Got the players. He had all of the ingredients. At one point he tried to get me. I was going to sign my last contract with the Spurs, and Angelo Drossos and I were at the Old San Francisco Steakhouse in San Antonio. No one else was there except us, and Drossos told me what the Lakers offered. "GG, uh, the Los Angeles Lakers want to give us three first-round draft picks for you to play with them. And I'm coming to you and asking you out of the respect I have for you. What do you want to do?"

He told me Buss called him to make him that offer. I said, "C'mon, man, I'm a Spur."

I said, "I'm signing here, and we gonna beat the Lakers." You can only imagine Spurs owner Angelo Drossos' face at the time and how proud he probably felt to have that kind of sense of loyalty. I'm not going to say that he loved me for that, but he loved what I represented in what we were trying to accomplish in San Antonio. I stayed to knock them off; it just didn't work. You play for the win, but you live for the challenge.

Now Drossos is dead. Dr. Buss is dead. So neither of them are here to verify this, but this is my story, and I have no reason to lie. I had an opportunity to go play for the Lakers. That's a fact. But for me and how I came up, I wanted to beat the Lakers—not join them. That wouldn't have been satisfying for me, so I refused to deal. Once I refused, Drossos said okay, and I signed my last contract with the Spurs that day.

Every owner didn't have his mentality, and you could tell. When you started looking around at who the Lakers had on their teams all of those years while he was owner it'll tell you. Just start looking at the talent. He was getting them, he was finding them, and he was paying them. Spencer Haywood played for him. Bob McAdoo played for him. He already had Kareem Abdul-Jabbar and Wilkes. He drafted Magic. Drafted James Worthy. He had Coop. He traded Norm Nixon for Byron Scott as a rookie. Mychal

Thompson, who was a No. 1 pick, played for him. Way back then Buss already knew better than most of how to put a winner together.

Same could be said about the Boston Celtics before the Lakers with Bill Russell and them. Red Auerbach knew. Sam Jones, K.C. Jones, John Havlicek, Don Nelson, Satch Sanders, guys who knew how to play their roles and win. They were building. That's what I felt we were doing in San Antonio: we were building. Especially after we got Artis Gilmore. Now no one was going to stop Jabbar; we knew that. But Gilmore could make things difficult for him. And he had "that other guy" from down the road where I come from in Detroit: Magic.

I loved the challenge, and that's what the Lakers brought. We went into their place and got some wins to let them know we weren't scared of them. We just didn't go in there long enough, often enough, and at the right times to get the crown. But winning and losing doesn't define who I am. It's still a game, it's a part of life, but it ain't life. I came up in an era where the challenge is just as, if not more, important than the win. We knew the Lakers had to go home and lay down after it was all over with us because we gave them all we had. Our philosophy was: "You mighta won, but you gonna go home and have nightmares about us." I know they went to sleep and woke up thinking about us. And I know it because I hear the guys saying it 40 years later. I hear Magic and them talk about us, I hear Coop and them talk about us, I hear Jabbar and them talk about us. I hear them when they talk about their championships and having to deal with us. That's rewarding enough for me. They knew we were there. They felt us.

I'm never doubting or taking anything away from my guys, but those guys, the Lakers, they just knew how to win. I think everything comes down to knowing how to win. Not saying that we didn't know, but something was missing. Something that didn't allow us to get over the hump with them. It may have been Magic. Ain't no question what happened to that organization once he got there. When you add it all up after his career, you see all of the accomplishments and see why he's top 50 all time. It makes sense. But his ability to be able to finish was his greatest asset and probably our biggest problem.

Being a student of the game, after I was done playing, I started thinking of different ways of how things could have gone, ways where we could have had different outcomes. Like with the Washington Bullets, we beat them, but we didn't finish them. Maybe they knew our gameplan, what we were going to do, how we were going to get there. No disrespect to Doug Moe or any of my teammates or anyone, but this is my own personal reflection on these losses and what goes through my mind when I think back on it. I'm looking at me first. I'm not looking at anyone else. I'm drawing my own painting. Doing my own second-guessing.

I truly feel we could've beaten the Lakers, but it's all hindsight though, and hindsight ain't worth a quarter. All it does is make you madder. But I've had the privilege to go over my career and dissect it and see where I could have gotten basketball's ultimate prize: a championship. But I didn't. And that hindsight reminds me in 1982 the Lakers swept us, beat us 4–0. In 1983 we got two games off of them, and they beat us in six games, which was the closest we got trying to go through them.

CHAPTER ELEVEN

FRANCHISE

My relationship with them is more than just flesh and blood.

When you think about it, I got to San Antonio in the early-mid 1970s, and the population was around 500,000 to 600,000. Now it's the seventh largest city in the country. So I've not only watched it grow, but I've also been a part of its growth. People walk up to me and say that I'm the reason the San Antonio Spurs are even here and they say it with conviction. They say the city grew because of me and that I'm a part of the reason for the city's growth—along with Red McCombs, Angelo Drossos, and the Holts. People tell me this all of the time. I'm not that vain to sit up here and say about the Spurs, "You know, y'all wouldn't be here without me." But I feel like I'm just one part of the foundation. That's kind of like how I am part of the foundation of the growth of the ABA, Nike, and the NBA. I've been here 46 years. I've seen every era of the Spurs organization. David Robinson's era. Tim Duncan's era. And obviously mine was the first. While I was going through it, I had no idea that I was going to be the root of an era. It's kinda like the ICEMAN poster. I had no idea it would be part of something special. Didn't see it, didn't expect it, didn't think about it. But I appreciated it. Fortunately, all of the Spurs owners have been local. So they all knew me and what I've meant to the franchise. And they have used me in different capacities to keep me connected to the franchise and the city, which I've been comfortable with.

People have asked if I feel the Spurs get enough credit for the role we played in inventing the transition, ball movement, high scoring, pace-and-space brand of ball that is being played now. Well, naw, we don't. But I expected us not to get it mostly because of geographically where we are. The big machine gotta sell where the big boys are at, and San Antonio, we're a small market. We're the Alamo. We're Davy Crockett. That doesn't sell. And it didn't sell until them boys stepped up and won five of them championships. And at the same time, the Spurs don't get the credit that they deserve for the impact and influence they had on the game, when you talk about powerhouses and winning. Because of where we are geographically, we never got the attention we probably should have, and that affected our placement in the bigger story of the game and the role we played in it because we were special.

And most of that credit should go to Doug Moe and Bob Bass. Even though Stan Albeck coached us for three seasons during that period, Moe was the one who told us, "If we get up a 100 shots a game, we're going to beat most people." That was our philosophy back then in the late 1970s, early 1980s. Get up shots. Push it up and score. And with Moe I had the green light, so I could shoot anytime I wanted to, and it benefitted my game. Mostly because I had so many tools, I was able to do a lot offensively because of the pace of the game. In that aspect I believe the Spurs had a great impact on basketball. Sorta like Steph Curry with the Golden State Warriors. He can shoot any time he wants. He can be laying on the floor and he can shoot it. If he's falling, he can shoot it. If he's going to the bathroom, he can shoot it.

I had a coach who emphasized shooting and pace. Moe would always say, "One thing I love about George Gervin is: he has the green light and he can shoot whenever he wants, but he don't take bad shots." The Denver Nuggets had a similar system. They played the same way and had the same philosophy in scoring, too. Alex English could score, Kiki Vandeweghe could score, David Thompson could score consistently. Every night you had to worry about one of them getting 40 on you and sometimes two of them in the same game. We were all runnin' and gunnin' on you.

People talk about pressure. I always look at my game and say, "Where was the pressure?" I was a scorer; that was my job. The other teams' job was to come and stop me. The pressure's on them. It was very seldom in that era where teams were based around guards. Our offense came through me, so I took the responsibility of the winning and the losing. And in the end, I always felt that we didn't stop people when we should have. We had the offensive power. We just didn't put an emphasis on making the stops we probably should have. We didn't have to be a great defensive team, but to me what separates champions from everyone else is that they stop other teams when they have to. They're up five or six points late in a game, and the other team comes down, and they hold them versus allowing a three-pointer to close the gap and shift that momentum. That's what Michael Cooper was for the Los Angeles Lakers. He's one of the ones who stopped us from getting to that next level. He was known for playing great defense, for hustling, and for talking stuff. Same with Draymond Green on the Warriors now. Those are the kinda players who give their teams a defensive identity and allow those teams to make those stops.

If you look at how basketball is played today, it's played very much the way we played it in the ABA. Just the style of play. Look who's winning now. The Warriors are playing the same way we did. But they found a way to use that style and win championships with it. I think about the impact we would have had on the game had we'd gotten to the Finals in 1979. Especially had we won it all. Back then that style of play was who we were, and no one else in the NBA was really playing like we were at the time. Had we won it all, we would have revolutionized the game much earlier. We're talking in the 1970s! When we came into the NBA, teams a lot of years were averaging 90 points a night. The Spurs came in averaging somewhere around 115 to 116 points a game. We picked up the pace and made it more entertaining, and the product becomes easier to sell. So the league itself became more interesting. When Bass switched me from forward to guard, it changed basketball from the aspect of redefining what a big two-guard was. I was the first big two-guard, I was winning scoring titles, I was shooting at a high percentage, and our team was winning. We changed the NBA.

* * *

Those last two seasons in San Antonio were tough for me. In 1983–84 our record was 37–45, and we didn't make the playoffs for the first time since we'd been in the NBA. Stan Albeck left as coach to take the Nets head coaching job in New Jersey, and his assistant Morris McHone came in and he was fired midway through the season after we started 11–20. And I was beginning to malfunction by then.

The next season the San Antonio Spurs hired Cotton Fitzsimmons as the new head coach. And that ended up not being a good hire. As for my situation, Alvin Robertson came in. He was an unbelievable athlete. He couldn't fit my shoes, but for the system that we wanted to run, it made sense for Robertson and Johnny Moore to start. They were two tough guards defensively, and then the Spurs could bring me in off the bench to attack offensively. But I didn't look at it like that, and we didn't have a coach who would explain it to me like that. In my mind I was protecting my legacy, and he came in to disrupt it. So it made me fight it more than accept it. Fitzsimmons was more of a my-way-or-the-highway kind of person. Direct. He had that kind of mentality, and I fought it. And I already know if he would have said to me, "Look GG, this is what I want to bring, and I'm coming to you first because I want you to buy into it. We got these two young, strong bulls in Alvin and Johnny, and I want to send them out there first and run the other teams to death, then put you in, and you lay 'em out, put all of those other teams to rest. This is how I think you'll be more valuable." That would have helped me. But the way he presented it didn't work for me.

And me being who I am, I was like, "Wait a minute, who you talkin' to? That ain't gonna work, buddy." I don't think he came at me the way a new coach should with a veteran like me. I probably was fighting that more than anything else. I didn't deserve that; that's what I was feeling. I didn't deserve to be talked to like that, even though it was his team and he's the new coach, but for all I'd done for that team and organization, I didn't deserve to be treated with that type of attitude. At one point I even said, "Hey, have I done everything you've wanted me to do?"

And he actually said, "Yeah, yeah, Ice, I gotta give you that. You have."

And I was like, "If you gotta give me that, then why don't you give me something else? Some respect."

Now, I'm not blaming Fitzsimmons by any means. It was still my choice to react the way that I did. The situation brought out that bad spirit in me, it took that humility away. And what's on the other side of that? Fight. Not turn the other cheek. It brought that East Side Detroit outta me. I mean, I was trying to get away from that, but it was still in me. And right then, I'm losing my humbleness. I was thinking I'd rather not play for him. And the Spurs ownership kept trying to get me to stay. Man, I think about that situation a lot. The Drossos wanted me to stay so bad. They gave me a bed of roses to lay in. But that fight was in me. I didn't want to hear it.

* * *

I'm sitting on about 30 acres out here right outside of San Antonio. All I do now is cut the grass, shoot some rattlesnakes, and wait for deer season. I wait for one of those axis or whitetail to come by so that I can get me some dinner. I harvest the deer so that I can eat it, not to put antlers on my wall. And I'm able to do that on my own property. I look at my life and say, "George Gervin, he's alright." Totally different than the kid who came from the streets of Detroit.

I like being regular. As regular as I can be. I know what the inner city did to me. I lived it, was a part of it, was able to get out of it, and ended up developing a life that I never knew existed. A life of calm and peace. I'm in no rush for anything anymore. I ain't in a hurry. I don't need that much anymore. I spend the rest of my days getting in touch with my own spirituality and enjoying this family that we've created.

From a basketball perspective, I'll drive by the AT&T Center or I'll watch a San Antonio Spurs game. Just being here from the beginning means something to me. When I was playing, all we were trying to do was win. Even though we never won it all, we built a winning culture. The next regime was able to come in and take what we did to the next level. And from that aspect, I'd have to say with the Spurs that's all because of ownership. Everything starts with ownership. They always wanted to win. A lot of franchises don't do that. Here they do. Because they've had winners, successful businessmen. Angelo Drossos was successful in his businesses, Red McCombs was successful in his businesses, and those were the two main owners, and they wanted to win because they knew winning brings attention. And they wanted attention for the city. So they did what it took to build that foundation up.

When you pull up Spurs on Wikipedia, they have a whole segment on there, "1976–1985: The George Gervin Era." I never looked at it until someone asked me how I felt about having an entire era named after me. That's humbling. We celebrated 50 years of the Spurs organization in 2022, and for me to have that type of impact upon the foundation, there's no other word but *humbling*.

When it comes to the Spurs, people always want me to talk about me the part I played. They want to hear me talk about the nine NBA All-Star Games, the four scoring championships in five years, the five times I was first-team All-NBA, the seven times I was All-NBA, the All-Star Game MVP in 1980, the Hall of Fame, but instead I always bring up the tree analogy. I give them an illustration and let them be the ones who determine what is the most valuable part of that tree that is the Spurs. Most people that I tell that to look at me and say, "Man, I ain't never heard of no shit like that before...but it makes all of the sense in the world."

My foundational relationship with the roots of the Spurs is almost spiritual. That's the beauty of it. Back then, when I came in, we weren't anything more than a \$2 or \$3 million franchise. We're worth \$2 billion now. Right now they're building a half-a-billion-dollar practice facility with all of the medical, nutritional help any team needs. When I came, when I played, we had 10 people in the office. *Ten people running the entire franchise!* Now there are between 270 and 300. That's what I've seen. And that's why Gregg Popovich ain't gone anywhere. Pop's a part of this growth, too. He knows. And Pop's a George Gervin fan. Again, he knows.

What I did on that court is already in the books. Every now and then, I get nostalgic and somctimes get sensitive about some of the narratives about my career and what some people say, but that's because I'm human. In reality, in my everyday, I'm past all of that. I'll let others play that game. For me, like my wife likes to say, "Game over."

I won four scoring titles in all. There are only two players, Michael Jordan and Wilt Chamberlain, in the history of the NBA who've won more than four, and only two others, Allen Iverson and Kevin Durant, besides me who have four. So yeah, I do realize that I accomplished some things in the game. Especially when I was in that San Antonio uniform. But those records and stats and accomplishments, they don't mean the same to me anymore. But they mean something to the organization, they mean something to the game. To hear David Robinson's Hall of Fame speech reminded me of that. I was one of his presenters. And what he said was mind-blowing. He talked about me and what I was to the franchise. When somebody else talks about you, the appreciation that they have for you, and the work that you put in, for me those moments are often mind-blowing. I can't think of another word that describes that feeling. After his career was over, he took the time to say how important I was for being the foundation of what his team and the franchise grew to be. Not everyone gets a chance to hear that. Brought tears to my eyes.

In December of 2021, I returned to Eastern Michigan, where I starred in college. *(AP Images)*

During my ABA days, I maneuver around Larry Kenon of the New York Nets on December 21, 1973. *(AP Images)*

We shot this iconic Nike poster in an icehouse in Seattle, and all I thought about was getting off that ice because I was freezing. But people still talk about it today, and I still sign those posters more than 40 years later. *(Iceman Poster provided by Nike, Inc.)*

I throw down a dunk against Bob Gross (30) and Johnny Davis (16) of the Portland Trail Blazers on February 21, 1978. *(AP Images)*

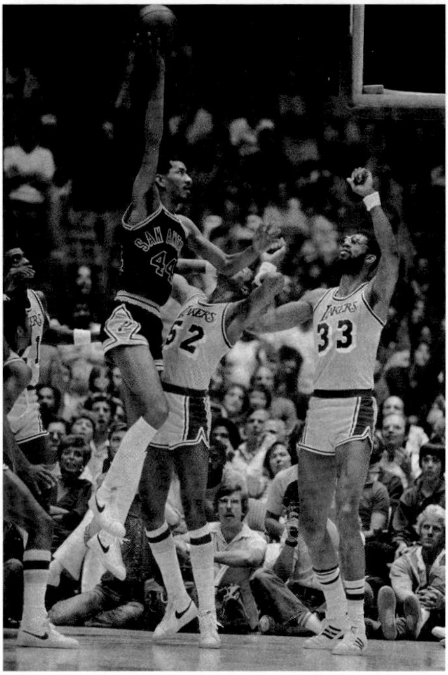

During the 1982 Western Conference Finals, I take a hook shot over Jamaal Wilkes (52) and Kareem Abdul-Jabbar (33) of the Los Angeles Lakers. *(AP Images)*

I back down Clint Richardson of the Philadelphia 76ers during a game in which I scored 43 points on December 21, 1983. *(AP Images)*

During my final year in the NBA, I go to the basket against Ken Bannister of the New York Knicks while playing for the Chicago Bulls in 1986. *(AP Images)*

The one thing I could do is finger roll. *(Getty Images)*

Joyce and I were quite the couple in our younger years. *(George Gervin)*

My son (Gee) and I chill on the water. *(George Gervin)*

In August of 1997, (from left to right) Connie Hawkins, Marvin Barnes, Julius Erving, Charlie Scott, and I pose for a photograph at the 30th reunion of the ABA. *(AP Images)*

For a roundtable discussion in 2004, I met with fellow NBA luminaries. In the front row (from left to right) are Willis Reed, Kareem Abdul-Jabbar, Bill Russell, Bill Walton, and Robert Parish. I'm in the back row next to Clyde Drexler, Rick Barry, Oscar Robertson, and Walt Frazier. *(AP Images)*

Nancy Lieberman, David Thompson, George Yardley, and I were inducted into the Basketball Hall of Fame in 1996. *(AP Images)*

I pose with my family (from left to right) son, George Jr. (Gee); son, Jared Gervin; daughter, Tia Gervin; and wife, Joyce Gervin. *(George Gervin)*

The kids at the George Gervin Academy mean everything to me. *(George Gervin)*

A Spur for life, I congratulate San Antonio Spurs guard Tony Parker after he helped defeat the Memphis Grizzlies in the Western Conference Finals to advance to the 2013 NBA Finals. *(AP Images)*

CHAPTER TWELVE

THE FINISH LINE

Everyone ain't ready for the finish line.

I was glad to retire from the NBA because I'd had my turn. But then I ran into that buzzsaw named Michael Jordan, and he was so good. I never felt envious or jealous, none of that, but I saw what was coming. Now I was older and not the same guy, but Jordan made it tough because you never wanted to admit that anyone was that much better than you at the time. Not while you're still in it, not while you still can ball. But I knew immediately he loved the game. I didn't ever have to question that. I knew who he was to the game at that time. His potential was scary. How he practiced was scary. He played like he practiced and he practiced like he played. Despite how good he was, I could tell that he was *in love* with this game. But I knew my time was over. Like one of those horses, I knew it was time to put me out to pasture, and that was hard for me to accept. So I got myself together a little bit and went over to Europe to play for a couple of years. That was great for me, that helped.

But I knew it was time for me to step away from the NBA. I didn't have the same desire anymore. I wasn't in love with it anymore. And I think I really fell out of love with it that year. I was on top of the game for most of my career, and sometimes it's hard to come down. I think about leaving the San Antonio Spurs and putting myself in that situation to be on the Chicago Bulls. I was with Cotton Fitzsimmons, and he had that other role he wanted me to play and I wasn't really ready to make that change. And fought it.

The owner of the Spurs, Angelo Drossos, he tried to do everything he could to get me to understand that he didn't want me to leave. Instead, I put him in a situation where he had to trade me. And I'm so sorry that I did that and that he's no longer here for me to tell him that. (Drossos passed away in 1997.) But I tell his kids that their dad loved me and that he didn't wanna trade me, but I really didn't give him any choice. But that's a lesson, too. You can only stay on top so long and when you realize when it's time to step down and you don't, that's a bad decision. And that was a bad choice for me to do to the Spurs franchise. My brain was malfunctioning; I can say it that way. Wasn't making good choices, and people don't make good choices when they aren't themselves. I let the situation throw me off my path. Because I never should have left San Antone. I should have been in one uniform, and they wanted me to be in one uniform. The Spurs did not want me to go. But I was fighting it. They felt that I was a big part of what this franchise was. Drossos told me at that time, "Man, just retire, and I'll give you half of your money this year and the other half next year." I was making $800,000. So I would've gotten $400,000 right then and then $400,000 the next year. He made it very attractive, but, I guess—and that's the only way I can put it, thinking back on it—I wasn't ready to hang it up. I saw the finish line and I wasn't ready to cross it. Wasn't ready to face it. So I ended up going to Chicago.

It really educated me in the sense that it made me truly realize you only can stay on top for so long. I don't care who you are. And when you outlive that time on top, it becomes a mental challenge and a mental health issue. You can't do what you used to do, but you still want those same accolades versus appreciating what you've done and taking that secondary role and still being effective. I fought that while I was also fighting the coach for how I felt he was disrespecting me. I was going through two battles at the same time—one external, the other internal. I probably could easily have stayed in San Antone, came off the bench, and been a Sixth Man of the Year. But that's where the mental health part comes into play and doesn't allow you to think like that. Has you thinking that you still supposed to be The Man. But when I pull back, I think maybe that's the way my basketball life was supposed to be: start my career with Julius Erving and end it with Jordan, two of the greatest to ever play this game. I like that aspect of it. I like to think about it that way because I'm the only one who can say he was able to do that.

If I'd come to the Bulls a year early, things may have been a little different with Jordan and me. My personality and his desire to beat everybody would have probably clicked differently. To have that one-on-one with him, I think that would have been special. Could have been similar to Doc and me, I believe. But Jordan had a year under his belt when I got there. He'd already developed his way of thinking and knew what he wanted to do. He was always about proving himself to be who he became. One of the best to ever do it. At the NBA 75, he was still challenging Magic Johnson. That's Jordan; he's going to be that way until he can't move anymore. Like in that ESPN documentary. *I bet I can throw this quarter closer to the line than you can.* That's just his personality. He don't mean anything by it; he just *that* competitive. I love a person being himself, and that's what made him who he was. And I never ever been caught up in the arguments about who's the best ever. I just don't think it's fair, but in his era, ain't nobody—nobody—did anything like him. And I ain't ever heard him say it, and that's what I love about him the most. He ain't the one saying he's the greatest ever.

I know my personality. I'm a fun-loving guy. To have a rookie like Jordan, shucks, I would have competed to see who could outshoot who. Accepting those challenges would've been fun. That's what I always enjoyed. And that's just how Dr. J and I were. It wasn't about winning or losing; it was about getting each other right and being good teammates. That's so important to me. I couldn't have accomplished a lot of things if my teammates didn't believe in me. I couldn't do it by myself. They knew to give me that rock, and I knew to give it to them, too. That's the thing: I could shoot whenever I wanted to, so I wanted my teammates to shoot some, too.

It's about how you handle the comedown. Because for so long we're up at a high. Not a drug high, a career high, a life high. On top. And I was at a high for a long time because I was one of the best. But then I was worn out. I made it through that year, but that was a tough year for me. And it really didn't have anything to do with basketball. It was just the end was coming. I was The Man of a team before and I was on another team where another guy is The Man, so I was able to see that. And I accepted it. It's not like I fought it. It was time to say good-bye to the game I loved. I didn't have the same desires. The love was dying. That's an emotional time. I knew I didn't have it anymore, and the way I went out was not the way I came in. How can you step down? Or how can you be put down? Those are your choices. If you get hurt, they put you down. The finish line hit me. I don't think I accepted the end of my career well. I didn't deal with it right.

I was in paradise where I was in San Antone. And the owner tried to make me realize it. But I couldn't because I was just thinking about me. And that's always the wrong move. For a lot of us athletes, when that time comes, a bad spirit takes over. We aren't ourselves. We're not making humble choices. Because when you make humble choices, that means you are thinking about someone else—not just yourself. And I say this as an educational piece for any young guys out there: anger shouldn't stop you from being yourself. Nothing wrong with thinking about you, but you gotta think about others, too. Throughout my career I thought about other people—not just myself—and that's why I probably had such a successful career with a team. All of my guys loved me because they knew I wan't selfish. They knew I always cared for them, too. But when you fight evil with evil, it seems like you always end up in a spot where you gotta keep fighting it. And then I become a Bull.

And then I had to deal with this '85 All-Star thing and them saying I'm jealous of Jordan. It just kept getting worse all because I took myself out of paradise. Took myself on another journey. The Bulls would be the last NBA franchise that I played for. Had I been thinking with my heart, I probably coulda stayed in San Antone another two or three years because they fired Fitzsimmons the next year anyway.

I think about the final NBA game I actually played in—Game Two versus the Boston Celtics in the playoff game where Jordan famously scored 63 points—and the role it's played in my career. I've always looked at it as another good indication that my turn had come to an end. I thought about my career during that game and how I used to put the ball in the basket and scored in all different kind of ways, and to watch young Jordan, who was doing it in a different, athletic way, really opened my eyes about being able to walk away from the game gracefully. You can only be on top for so long, and seeing Jordan in that game reinforced in me that I knew my time was up.

Of all things I regret most is the part of losing myself. I could have made a whole lotta bad choices being in that frame of mind. After crossing that finish line into retirement, that's when I think you can start having tough times. I went from an All-Star in '85 to retiring in '86. It happened quick. That's basically when that drug thing occurred with me, right at the end. I mean, you're coming down from a high—a natural one of being one of the best and coming down from that. And everyone ain't ready for the finish line. You already proved that you were one of the best to ever do it, but for some reason, you can't figure out how to let go. I fault myself for taking most of the things in my heart and putting them in my mind. I don't regret going to the Bulls. Some good things happened while I was there; some bad things happened. I don't blame Fitzsimmons for anything; it was just the situation. I was

36 years old at the time. I started pro ball when I was 20. Long time. And I was still on top just not *at* the top. So I knew and agreed that it was time. I just didn't handle it like I know I could have. I ain't perfect. I'm still appreciative that I was able to overcome the things that were bothering me, the choices that I made, the people who I associated with. A lot of them are no longer here because of things that we indulged in, and I hope I've told their story.

My story continued in Europe after I was done with the Bulls. Playing over in Italy when I did was what I needed. It was the end of my NBA career, but I could still play a little bit. So they still got to see a little bit of what I could do. After I was over there for a while, the owner of the team I was playing for came to me, speaking to me in Italian, and said: "When is the real Iceman going to show up?" And I had to laugh because I was averaging 26 points a game.

Playing in Europe was the best thing to happen to me. Period. I took my wife over there, took our kids. They got a chance to go to international schools over there, got a chance to be around kids from all over the world. It was a whole different exposure, which was a plus for them. It also gave us a sense of history of the world. We got to see the Vatican and listen to the pope every Wednesday and Sunday. We were able to be amongst the thousands and thousands of people going to St. Peter's Basilica. Going to see the Sistine Chapel, looking up at that beautiful ceiling, things like that change you. Having those types of experiences can change the way you look at life. I know a lot of guys who are on their way out in the game. For them, going overseas and playing could be a true joy for them. But they have to allow it to happen.

I had an African cook, and she would cook us these different African meals that were nothing like we'd ever tasted, and we got them every day. She cooked us some greens and steak, and I'm still trying to figure out how she got that to taste so good. I can't remember exactly what country she was from in Africa, but she lived in Italy. So she was cooking her own food based on her own African customs, but she was also cooking us unbelievable Italian food. I still haven't had any food like that in my life. We lived in this big ol' house. So my stage was set as far as our living quarters were concerned.

Basketball-wise, I was playing in the big leagues there, playing for Virtus Roma. I was playing against players like Bob McAdoo and players like that and playing in front of 18 to 19,000 people. I couldn't ask for anything better at that time. So my experience over there—especially in Italy—was so great. Even though our team never won it all, I had an opportunity to really enjoy my time over there. It was really a blessing. Think about it: I played in the ABA and NBA 14 years. So for 14 years I'm up on a real high, a basketball high, and it helped me come down. It also helped me deal with some of those demons I was dealing with. I was coming down off the two highs I was on. So it was perfect. I had one game a week. We played on Sunday at 5:00 PM. We played 30 games a season. So that's 30 Sundays. We practiced more than we played. For me, there's only really one way to describe it: it was beautiful. It also gave me a beautiful perspective spiritually. It became that thing that held me and our family together. It was another ingredient that helped me be here to tell this story today.

But one year in Italy was enough. That's all I needed. My feet were back on the ground, and the family and I came back home to America. The Houston Rockets tried to get me to play for them in the playoffs. But I was done. I could still play, but I was half of me at that point. Now I did go back and play in Spain for a year. I played for Manresa and got to enjoy that and see all of Spain, but I was at the end at that point. Looking back on that time, knowing what I know now that I didn't know back then—because I didn't know Jehovah then and I didn't know how he loved not just me but all of his creations—I know he had a hand in me playing over in Europe at that time in my life because that ended up saving me. The way I was? It had to be something greater than man. Those drugs have the power to take you out and make you not be you no more. I got lost; I'm sorry that I did. But I got found, too, and I'm not sorry about that. And one of the experiences in my life that helped me find myself again was being able to experience another part of the world and playing ball over in Europe for those two years. It gave me a sense of whole.

CHAPTER THIRTEEN

NO LONGER GEORGE

I was no longer George.

I turned 70 on the 26th of April 2022. In real life that's retirement. You're supposed to be going out to the water, appreciating what I call "Jehovah's creations." I'm trying to take in all the marvels of what we're dealing with on this beautiful Earth that we live on. I'm trying to put the work in, stay with something good, so that when I'm done with the kids, I let them take care of me. I done took care of them. Now, they've gotta take care of me. I kid, but that's kind of the cycle of life. That's the way it works.

Before we were married, my wife used to work at Woolworth, and I used to drive over there and say to her, "I need 20, honey." And she'd loan me $20. And I'd tell her later, "You made an unbelievable investment." I knew I had something special just by the introduction. Even with all we've been through, it still turned out happily ever after. Because I can still make her laugh after 45 years. And we can still talk about yesterday, today, and the future—that's what we have in common. This is the part of life that I feel is most rewarding. The family.

In our jobs as entertainers, a lot of professional athletes and their wives don't stay together. The influences and the choices that you make separate you. Sometimes it gets so bad that it tears up everybody. When I say everybody, I mean it tears up the wives, the husbands, breaks up the kids. And it can get terrible. We forget that God is the one that made the arrangements for marriage. So if that's the case, then that's what He wants. A lot of people get married for love, but it's bigger than that. It's all spiritual, which a lot of us don't research. And really the only thing that can save your marriage is researching the bible's understanding of what marriage is—how to maintain it, how to live by the words in there. A big reason why so many break up is because it's so easy to do without a foundation beyond just love for each other. It's easy to say "bye." It's harder to say, "Naw, we gonna work this out. I screwed up, I'm sorry." To me, there's another force out here that influences us to do some things that we shouldn't do. That's that competition between bad and good, one that we always got to deal with. It truly affects our lives. So I'm thankful to still be with mine for 45 years through some of the turbulent times and troubled times. We were still able to overcome them. And it's a testament to Joyce, my wife. She held it all together.

Because I was gone. I was gone. But she still had that invisible string on me. Well, I won't even call it a string…a chain. Because you couldn't break it. A string you can cut. And that's what she had on me. She had our babies, I knew she loved me. And I got out there, I got lost. Started medicating.

Once you do that, your brain starts malfunctioning. I was out of character, I was no longer George. But that chain was the anchor; that's what was holding me down. I needed an anchor, still do. I don't need to go bobbin'. And in that world I was living in, just look at how many we've lost because they didn't have a foundation. According to Mark Kreidler of ESPN.com, the divorce rate among all professional athletes is estimated at between 60 and 80 percent. According to a 2009 *Sports Illustrated* study, 60 percent of NBA players go bankrupt within five years after leaving their sport. Every time I see somebody struggling with drugs, alcohol, or mental health issues, it actually hurts my heart. Because I know how tough it is. And I only know how tough it is because I've experienced it. I done dealt with a lot. With drugs I had my bout with them.

That's the thing I think about a lot. I debated whether to include my struggles with drugs in this book. Then I realized it's about the recovery; that's where the story is. During those times you lose yourself because you aren't you anymore, but then can you find yourself? That's the key. It brings tears to my eyes sometimes when I think about those times because it wasn't me. It was that powerful influence that we—athletes, entertainers—are living under. And if you ain't in love with somebody, man, you can be in big trouble with your life. You can get lost. And then try to start it all over again.

Most entertainers and athletes, especially in the system, they get married two, three times. They never figured it out, they never figured out what their marriage is really all about. Joyce let me figure it out. That's why I'm so thankful for my wife, for the love she has for me and our family because she was like a lioness with the kids. She'd cut my head off when it came to that. I, of course, don't mean that literally. I mean it symbolically. And you know you gotta real one when they're like that.

When we separated—this was my plan, though some people think I'm nuts—I had it arranged that we were always going to get back together. Joyce didn't know that was my plan. This was October 1984, and we were back married seven months later in 1985. I thought it was better to re-court her than to try and fight that demon that separated us. My boys told me that I had a lot of nerve doing it. I told them, "This is what I gotta do to make it whole again."

I always felt I was smooth enough to recapture her. When things get so bad sometimes, you know there's only one or two ways you go. You can go on and blow it all off like a little cloud, and the big wind comes along and blows it all away where you can no longer find it, or you can realize that things have happened that mean you have to make a change in order to recapture something you have lost. And that was my whole goal because things in my life had gotten so twisted and turned by the choices that I was making. I realized it! And I knew it wasn't her. I knew it was me. So I had to get myself together. So, I had to take the risk of losing it all to gain myself, to get myself back together, to recapture what I lost. And that's what I did. And she still had faith in me during that time. That's a Black woman! They got that hard kinda love. That's what you need. That's what I needed. If I'd had a soft woman who let me get away with what I wanted to do, then I never would have recovered. I needed someone to fight me back. I needed to go get my own self together. And I took the steps to get that done.

I always thought about my dad when it came to my marriage. My dad wasn't with me and didn't spend any time with me. I didn't want that for my family. The pain I was putting her and the kids though and how I would live with that concerned me. I never lost sight of them and how what I was doing affected them. My dad was an alcoholic, my granddad was one, my uncle was an alcoholic, so it's been a part of my life. My uncle didn't recover. My granddad did. So I had examples on both ends. If I kept going like that, I was going to destroy myself, my family, and my legacy. I wouldn't have been recognized as one of the 75 greatest if I'd kept going in the direction I was going, which was secondary because I didn't care anything about that at the time. It was my family. I couldn't let my kids go to school and have other kids roll up on them saying, “Hey your dad, yeah, he was a great ballplayer, but, man, he was an alcoholic, drug addict.”

That’s hard for a kid to deal with. It’s hard for a wife. Maybe harder. She knew the backstory. She saw it, had to live with it. The kids just saw me and they didn’t understand. They just knew I was in pain and they were, too, because I was taking them through it. But she had to deal with it. But I always felt that God was in my life and He loved me even when I wasn’t showing that I loved Him back. Little did I know then that He was there with me all along. Because He knew my heart. My wife knew my heart. They already knew what kinda person I was. Even though I was just lost.

I was making bad choices and hanging around people who were also making bad choices. They weren’t necessarily bad people, but I was making bad choices by associating with people who didn’t have anything in common with me except getting drunk and getting high. Then it became a pattern. So then I was on that road to destruction, another form of suicide. I didn’t understand it while I was in it. There’s no clarity. I was malfunctioning. What was right was wrong to you, and what was wrong was right. And it became a mental health issue. I was fighting myself from the inside, and that’s how people end up killing themselves. Man, this whole thing gave me good insight into how suicide happens. It gets you so depressed, and you are medicated, and then it makes you want to go up on a bridge and jump off. I bet most of times on your way down you're trying to grab something because that ain't what you really wanted to do. That's how lost you can be. And really you are begging for help. At the same time, this other evil spirit doesn't want you to get it. That's the fight, and it's a dangerous fight.

The distractions are always there. I'm the perfect example of being distracted. It can happen to the best. For a lot of us brothas in the '70s and '80s, drugs and alcohol were big. I'm so glad I got out of that. But what makes people think today's star is going to be better at avoiding that than we were? They got more money, they got more time on their hands for isolation—and isolation ain't good for anyone—and when you make a $100 million, you are isolated because you're in a rare group.

I stopped beating myself up about that part of my life a long time ago. Because I know that wasn't me, and it's hard to keep holding that against myself. While I was going through the process, though, I could get mad because I knew what it was doing to me and I couldn't stop. It's like smoking cigarettes. I didn't start smoking until after my career. And I never liked cigarettes! Ain't nothing good about it, but you can't stop. It becomes intertwined in your life. Get up in the morning, I need a Kool. I drink my coffee, I need a Kool. I take a dump, I need a Kool afterward. I have sex, I need a

Kool. I used to tease my wife, "Wow, honey, I was smelling like this?" And she'd just look at me and roll her eyes.

But that's part of what I was going through. And that's why I'm so proud to be on the other side of that now. And some of my guys ain't, some of them still out there doing the same thing. Still caught up in it. And I know they're not happy. How could they be? I know what it does to you. I know the reality. But what I can't do is look down on them. I gotta instill my own little experience. I ain't going to ever say to someone, "You should quit that stuff." I instead have to be a good example because being a good example is better than telling somebody what they need to do. Because I can tell the same story to them they are living right now, but they know it. Once an alcoholic or drug addict, we're always going to be one. We're always one step from relapse.

While I was in it, I hated myself. I hate what it did to me.

Every time I see a movie star or an athlete have to struggle with that, it breaks me down because I know that journey that they're on. And I know how hard it is. I know what it does to you. I know where they at and I know what it's going to take to get that out of them. They're going to have to have some sorta spirituality. Because that demon don't play, and when you're in it, that demon got you. And you won't know it until you do some spiritual research. Until that you don't know who got a hold to you. I knew it was bigger than me at that time. And you can't beat him unless you got some spirituality. He's the God of this whole system, and I was praying to Him. Every time I was partaking, I was praying to Him. I needed His help. But that demon knows how to put things in your face, knows how to do things to you to make you just cheat people and life. Every day there are people who say, "I ain't gonna drink no more" or "I ain't gonna do this no more," and the enemy is saying: "We'll see." He knows how to win because he's doing it for a long time.

In *The Last Dance* documentary, I heard Michael Jordan talk about his first two years in the league and say, "Man, there was a lot of cocaine on our team." I just laughed. Yeah, there was a lot of cocaine in that era—period. It wasn't just your team, buddy. It was prevalent, and we were great stool pigeons then. Had everything, and money-wise we were needin' nothin'. But that goes to show you how if you don't have an understanding of where you are in your life, that money thing can be your detriment. I could afford anything I wanted. That was the era. Am I glad I went through it to be where I am today? Yes, because in losing myself, I found myself. That's the key. Sorta reminds you of that protected kid who hasn't been out, ain't experienced anything in the world, then you let him free. Them the ones you lose.

I was caught up in it for a few years, the last couple of years. At the end. But one of the best choices I made was not going to Los Angeles to play for the Lakers. Beating them instead of playing for them was one of the main reasons, but the other was what would have happened with my life off the court in L.A. That's what frightened me. Being in Sodom and Gomorrah is how I saw it. Not going to L.A. was probably one of the greatest moves I ever made. I sacrificed wins for life. At the time I was already in it, not deep but still enough to know that if I went to play in Los Angeles, my life would probably end. Knowing that, what the hell would I want to play there for? And I got a family. I thought about all of that. That would not have been a good fit for me. Now, it would've been a good fit if I sold my soul, but I was never going to sell my soul. Not like that. I would've been in a world that would have gobbled me up. I already knew that. I knew that from visiting there all of these years. So when I'm talking about not wanting to win at all costs, this is what I mean. A championship's not worth that to me. Not if that's how I had to get it and where I had to play. I'm not choosing a win over my soul. In the end the greatest gifts you can have are your sanity and your family. In Los Angeles at that time, I knew if had I gone, I was going to lose both.

I was hurtin' inside, and probably no one really knew that but me. So what I did was medicate. I tried to stop hurting. This world was praising me, and I definitely didn't need that. Because with all I had, all that that I accomplished, there was still something missing. I still wasn't happy. Fair or unfair, the world still narrated my career. What kind of fulfillment was I getting? Well, it wasn't the kind at the time I was looking for. But the lifestyle of the league back then allowed me to seek a fulfillment that I didn't need. Plus my pride. When I was in Chicago, I was in pain. I knew I should've still been in San Antonio for my last year in the NBA, but that pride hurt me more than anything down the stretch. It brought about a lot of pain, and the medicine I chose to use to try and make it go away was the wrong kind. If I had gone a more spiritual route to ease my pain, I know the pain would have subsided with me having a better understanding about pride and jealousy and envy, the things that make you turn to drugs.

When Marvin Gaye was singing about "Flying high in the friendly sky without ever leavin' the ground," and "I go to the places where danger awaits me," that always emotionally touched me because I knew what he was talking about. I was living it.

* * *

I knew what I was doing. The people around me, my wife, Coach Merriweather, all of my guys, my circle, were praying for me. They knew. And I knew I needed help. Joyce kept saying, "you need to go and get help." I kept hearing her voice. It got to a point where I wasn't worried about what I was going to lose. Because if I kept living the way I was living, I was going to lose me. I wasn't living the truth. The stress and anxiety of living that lie—and the pressure that's on someone who's addicted to something and how it infects the other people in their lives—finally got too heavy, and I knew that if I didn't do something, I was never going to find me again. I said to myself, *It's my turn*. Then randomly with nothing planned and no one around, one day I picked up the phone and called John Lucas and said, "Hey, man, I'm ready."

I rehabbed at Lucas' treatment facility in Houston. He and I were together. He was slipping a little bit then. His situation, I think, had a lot more impact on him than most. I knew Lucas real well. He was my teammate my last year with the San Antonio Spurs. I always liked him. He's smart with a good personality, so when it was time for me to seek help, he was the one I decided to go to. He knew, too. All he said to me when he answered the phone was, "You ready, Ice? I'm here."

He knew I was sick. But he also knew that until you know you're sick, then it ain't gonna work. And anytime you are dealing with treatment, you gotta go in for yourself. I knew I was going to lose my wife if I kept going like this. So I went there to clean myself up. Get my life back together. One of my guys came to pick me up in San Antonio and drove me up there. I saw Lucas, we went to a restaurant, ate real good, and then I went in.

When I went behind those doors at Lucas' place, I had to go up an elevator. That's when I *knew.* So once you go in and sign in and then get on that elevator, that elevator door closes, and there ain't no outs. You're stuck. And if you argue or fight, they put you in a straightjacket and put you in the suicide room. And the suicide room is all padded. You can't break anything, you can't bust you head, you can't do anything but settle down. I saw that and I said, "Oh well." I can laugh about it now. And for me recovery was fun. Lucas' approach to use physical fitness to get you back as a form of rehab was incredible because he was real serious about recovery. No nonsense. And he was the type of guy who made you quit if you weren't all of the way in it. We used to argue and fight all of the time, but it was all outta love. That brotha there, he was true to his mission, and that mission was to get me back to the other side. I don't know what I would have done without him. Because when those doors closed behind me, that was the beginning of closing that part of my life out. That's another reason I know there is a God. He's the only one who could have saved me at that time. Not my wife, not any of my people in my circle. Jehovah, as I know now, gave me the strength to give myself a chance.

Lucas would come and get me every morning at 5:30. And we'd go work out. He had this old man who he worked with named Doc, who was also into physical fitness, who had like a mom and pop fitness shop on the facility. The shop had everything in it you needed to work out. Weights. Benches. And then Lucas had a hill, a man-made hill, that we used to run up. So we'd run up the hill forward and do what we called "eight across." That's eight times up forward, then we'd walk down. Then we'd run up eight times backward, then walk back down. Then we'd frog jump up. The routines were unbelievable. Then I'd come back and I'd do my programs. I'd always go to Alcoholics Anonymous (AA) or Narcotics Anonymous (NA), and I'd have my circle where I talked with others. And I'm a relationship guy, so that helped me feel connected to others. It was the train I decided to get on to get myself together and I liked it…and it worked. I stayed there about 90 days. I stayed in the program about 30-something days then stayed in the aftercare program another 60-something days. I enjoyed it because I saw my life coming back.

I found myself when I was in recovery. I was cutting away from Ice. I became George again. I heard Beyonce say sometimes she's Beyonce and other times she's Sasha. That has more meaning than people think. They say it's your alter ego. Yeah, it's also one thing you can lose yourself in. For a while I was "Ice." I always wanted to be George. But I got tagged "Ice." Ice wasn't me. Ice was the one you could control; George controlled himself. But Ice was the alter ego, so it's almost like I was playing a role even while most of my life I was staying true to myself. And when you do that, it's harder to be you. I never liked being up front, never in my life. I never liked sitting in the front row, I never liked being in VIP. I'd rather sit in the back, I'd rather sit in the middle. I always wanted to be with and amongst my people, not separated from them. Those 8:00 AM to 5:00 PM guys, I was always comfortable around them. I never wanted people to think that I thought I was something or someone special. I hated that. But the things I was doing, it made "Ice" take center stage. And that's who went through all of that hell. It wasn't George. I was trying to find George. George was a lot more humble, a lot more loving.

Jerry West wrote me a letter when I was going through it. He told me to get well. I'll never forget it. I wish I could find that letter because it meant so much to me at that time. Those kind of things, those uplifting life experiences—people just don't know that the few words of encouragement that you can give someone and the impact those few words can have on somebody's life. It can change their lives or help change their lives. Those things are proof that it's more than just ball because I never forgot it.

A lot of players, who had successful careers, didn't recover. They aren't talked about anymore. Larry Drew. I think he was one of the baddest forwards to play the game, but he had issues. We lost a few of them. Fast Eddie Johnson. In that aspect, looking at it in that way, basketball did help. If you lost everything, if you're under a bridge, who's going to talk about you? Who's going to talk about the accomplishments you had for all of that hard work you put in your whole life? They can't take it from you, but they can act like it never happened. And we got kids. You don't want your kids hearing for the rest of their lives, "Yeah, yeah, your dad was all that, but he's under a bridge." I owed them better than that. Plus, I wanted to be in their lives. And the only way you can be in their lives is to get it together, brotha! Get yourself together. It worked out for me in that aspect. All of my kids love me to death. They love me for me. That's the love I want, that's the love I gave them. That's what we raised them for: we love them, and they love us. So, I got that. You know, I beat my wife up—figuratively obviously not literally—but she stuck with me. I want to make her happy while she's still here for making that sacrifice for our whole family.

Success comes from having great supporters like my family. That's the beauty of it. A lot of time we see how successful we've become but don't give our wives enough credit. I look at my wife, and she dealt with a lot with me. For her to get back to that man she fell in love with, she's deserving of all the accolades she should be getting. That's why I said, "I do." It took me a while to get there. My childhood, my mom and dad's situation, made me cautious. But that's the beauty of it, though, because I am thankful and happy with who I married. She's still a strong, Black woman from a big family. Met her on her first day of college. I was a sophomore; she was a freshman. On her birthday. We had a little history in high school because she went to a rival school, and our schools would play each other. She knew of me, but I didn't know anything about her until I met her at Eastern Michigan. And been with her pretty much ever since.

I just wanted to get over that hump. I didn't like that life I was living. It was scary and dangerous, and I had everything to lose with nothing to gain. And I didn't want to live like that—no more. It was tough on Joyce. I know I scarred her. That wasn't my normal me. She was helpless. But fortunately for me she was spiritually strong. She was a Jehovah Witness, and our kids were raised as Jehovah Witnesses. Her being a Jehovah Witness and understanding the bible teaching saved us. It gave her that comfort to deal with me and what I was putting her through. She talked to God through it. That's the only way I know she could have survived. I tell my daughter, "You better marry someone that has some spiritual understanding."

Love ain't enough. Just love ain't gonna hold up. You gotta know why you're getting or got married, then you gotta know what marriage is. There are times when it's too hard, too many things pulling you all apart. You need that proxy, that spirituality to be that glue. Something stronger than just love. Other than that it can be easy to throw up your hands and be done with everything. And you can get tired of her, too. For the wrong reasons. You're not giving yourself the opportunity to understand that the beautiful part of marriage is not you and her. It's the spiritual bond.

My favorite scripture is 1 John 5-19: "We originated with God, but the whole world lies in the power of the wicked one." It tells you: yeah, God created us, but in this system, it's run by the wicked, which doesn't want anything but turmoil and ugliness. That's why man can't govern himself. But I'm glad I have spirituality and a spiritual foundation. And I didn't get mine until later in life because I was so distracted. The world telling me how good I am. A lot comes with that. A lot of stress and strain. And if you don't have a spiritual foundation, you gonna have more than just headaches.

CHAPTER FOURTEEN

MENTAL HEALTH

I'm still talking about the system, man.

Things began to get clear to me once I retired. I was so lost in the world with ball. And not because I didn't respect the spiritual appetite that I had, but once everything was over, it was a scary time. They always say, "Plan ahead. Plan for retirement." Well, you might have a lot of money, but you still don't know how you are going to feel. And I was so in tune with the game. After my last game, I cried because I knew I was done. It was an unbelievable load off of me. People ask me, "Ice, would you want to do it over again if you had to do it all over again?"

I say, "Hell naw!"

I'd get me a job or something where I could come home every day and take care of my wife and my children, get me some land, grow my own vegetables, raise my own cattle, grow my own food. That's what I would do. Because that world there, that basketball world I come from, almost killed me. That world can swallow you up. Why would I want to do that again? And I didn't get my spiritual base until my last few years. I was so distracted. I didn't think I needed anything, but I needed *everything*. The game and fame can get you thinking we don't need nothin' because we got money, fame, and got people drooling over you and wooing you. There's temptation all around you so you can have your choice of anything. C'mon, who really wants that life? I say, a fool. I've lived it, want no parts of it twice. I know the drive that I had in me from playing that game of basketball. But I would have that same drive to take care of my family with a regular job.

Being a sports figure ain't all what it seems to be. In this job you can only stay on top so long. When we stretch it out, we hurt ourselves. I've heard the phrase, "We are living in a culture of idol worshippers." Man, that got to me when I heard that. It means we're living in a culture where they idolize idols. Athletes, entertainers, statues, false prophets. All of the things that the God, which I love, is totally against. That's kinda scary because it's so true. The scripture tells you to not bow down to idol worshippers—and we're in a culture where that's all they do.

I used to get a little disappointed if a guy walked past me didn't recognize me for being a ballplayer. But the league doesn't sell us, and then you have new people coming in who don't know anything about us, who haven't done any research. They just knew someone who got them a job in the game. They don't know any real history of the NBA. Just look at some of these general managers who don't know anything about the history of this game, but they're in control. How can our history be saved if no one is up there talking about it? And that's where a big part of what's going on rests.

Living in this system ain't no joke. There's so much against you. We have things that are working for us, but I still think there's so much pulling at us that we have to deal with. That creates another form of mental health. Denzel Washington and Tyler Perry were there at the Oscars to hold Will Smith after the situation with Chris Rock and they told him, "Hey, brotha, that ain't you. Yeah, we at the top, but we got to stop that enemy who's running this system. That's the one who's trying to get you. Rock is not the problem. It's bigger than that."

We call it mental health in the world we live in, but we know there's a bigger enemy out there that impacts all of us, and it has the power to make us all go dark. Look at gymnast Simone Biles or tennis player Naomi Osaka. They stepped forward and dealt with it. That takes strength.

Mental health is big in our society. We continue to see it every day, and it's getting worse and worse. We're starting to be able to see it in areas that used to be guarded. Like, once we saw the Smith debacle, it makes you realize that it's everywhere. At all levels. It don't matter. Even the people who are supposed to be running these countries, they have some real mental health issues. *And we depend on them?* We see what they do to people when they don't agree with them. I'm still talking about the system, man. But I can't help not to talk about it. Because I know more about it from my own studies. The only defense we have against the system is understanding and to not get caught up in it to where it kills you or takes your freedom away.

There's a lot of people who need help out here. And when you don't get help, you don't have any hope. And when you don't have hope, most times you don't have or you lose your consciousness and capacity to care. But you still have choices. And you usually make the bad ones when you got no conscience.

* * *

I'm a Jehovah's Witness. I've been around people of that faith probably half of my life. My wife has been a Jehovah's Witness for over 30 years. She raised our kids as Jehovah's Witnesses. I have friends who have been talking to me for years; some I've even studied the faith with. One of them went to college with me. But I never really took the interest early on, but I'd go to Memorial. I've been going to Memorial—which is the observation of the Lord's Evening meal once a year—for Jehovah's Witnesses for probably 25 to 30 years. They call it the "Passover." So, I knew about God, but I never researched to find out who He was. And as I studied, I gained a greater understanding of the fleshy desires that is the makeup of us as humans, and then there's a spiritual desire, an appetite. And all those years I never really fed my spiritual appetite. At 68 years old, that's when I started studying to feed my spiritual appetite on becoming a Jehovah's Witness. That's when I started going to bible study and going to Kingdom Hall. I was learning—learning about the faith through my own research and gaining an understanding and finding out through their faith that God had a name: Jehovah.

And it was that part that really intrigued me. That allowed me to pray to a God that has a name. I discovered how I was directly praying. And that helped me a lot. It gave me a sense of clarity. The best way I can explain it is like a friend once gave me an example. Say you gotta dog, and the dog is sitting in the corner. Now the dog has a name, but you say, "Hey, dog, come here." Now the dog will probably just turn around and look at you and go back to what he or she was doing. But if you say, "Hey, Bruno," he'll pop his ears up and he'll come to you. So I use that as an illustration to how my personal relationship with Jehovah is and how God now having a name to me changed my communication with God. Through this I also came to believe that Jehovah translated the bible in a way for me to better understand my relationship with God and for me to have a better way to deal with this world. Through prayer I directly talk to Him, and through His words in the bible, He communicates with me. I have faith in that, and that's why I decided a few years ago to dedicate my life to Jehovah. Had my personal prayer to Him and was baptized on January 23, 2022.

As human beings we a lot of times do things out of habit. My mom was a Baptist, and most people religious-wise follow after their parents. But whether you follow your parents or not, you as an individual have to have your own personal relationship with God. But a lot of people never get to the point where they understand that. I've always believed you should find out things for yourself. Do your research, find out what is best for you. Through my own research, I found through Jehovah's faith and interpretation so many helpful and encouraging scriptures and messages that helped me give a better life. It helped me become whole. Helped my understand this system we live in that is not going to last, but there is a new system, and we have the opportunity to live the way God created us to live and for man to one day inherit the Earth and live forever.

I have a different understanding of how I see the world and how I see it going. As an older man, I have a better understanding of who's running this system, and that's because of my studying. Some people believe in the devil, and some don't; some people believe in Satan, and some don't. But I would ask someone: if Satan was ruling the world, what would the world be like? I would just want to hear their answers.

Most would probably say that would be like it is now. So my belief is that if we are living within an influence that is that powerful—the same system that's been working for centuries—to make people hate one another, to pit us against each other, to divide us and watch us conquer ourselves. How do we change if we can't change it?

Just look at our game. The biggest thing currently is who's the G.O.A.T.? That's nothing but separation. And the system got us falling for it. If you got an ego, you're going to say, "It's me." And I laugh and say, "Oh yeah? Is it that important to you? To say I was the best to *ever* do it? For real?" We're all just in the top 75 or the top 50 or the top whatever. But they keep comparing LeBron James and Michael Jordan. And I get asked all the time, "Ice, who do you think?" My answer is I don't care because they're both a part of that group I'm in. Some might think that's no kind of answer. But what I've figured out is that it's all separation. By design. That's the tool that evil uses to keep people separated. I'm not falling into that trap. Now they're going to keep the story going, but all the story is going to do is continue to separate people. That's why I put up the narrative about us all being equal.

In that interview I did with Bill Simmons in 2014 on his *BS Report* podcast, I did say I felt Kareem Abdul-Jabbar was the greatest of all time, but I also said I was biased because that's who I played against. I said the same thing about Dr.

J. when he asked me the greatest of my era. But I'm sincere in saying I don't care because it doesn't matter and I see that there's no good intention or purpose in the foundation of that question. What I *do* care about, though, is these brothas playing this game being able to get along. I want them to stop thinking about the game they're playing and instead about the help that they could be giving to some of these younger men and babies out here picking up a basketball wanting to be them. I want them to keep them from fighting amongst themselves and saying who's the best because all that does is make the younger generation coming up beat their chests, walking around saying, "I'm better than you." Trying to be in a G.O.A.T. conversation as opposed to working on just being great. You gotta be wise to do that. We gotta be wise to teach them that.

People need to research to find out why it's really like this. Why is this system set up to separate even on small things like who's the greatest, so that we're always against one another? It's beyond prejudice, beyond Black and White, ethnicity, and all of that. Way beyond that. There's such a fight within. Without some form of spirituality, I'm not sure we're ever going to find a solution.

Is it worth it? What we put ourselves through to reach these certain levels of our careers. I've been asked that question a lot. I've come to the belief that it is worth the part of being able to endure and to have that success in something. But for life? You lose something. I say that with passion. It's not that you can't regain it or find it again, but most of us don't. It takes a lot out of you, and a lot of us lose the most precious things we have—and that's our families. I was asked once in my daily bible study, "If I put my sport up versus my families, which one would I choose?" And I'm talking this is after the fact, after I knew everything, after I went through it. And I chose my family. So that means I might lose a lotta money, I might lose the celebrity. So am I losing a lot? No. Our families are our lives, part of our creations. My family is an institution created by God through my marriage. And percentage-wise we run the strong risk of losing that by becoming professional athletes. That drive to reach that level takes something from you. I'm telling you. Just look at Tom Brady, and what he just went through. So in the end, what do we want? What should I choose? Because I know if I choose this life, I might lose my babies, my kids because I won't be able to nurture them the way they should be nurtured and raise them and give them something that's going to help them deal with this crazy world we bring them into because I'm putting all of myself into this game.

I'll tell you how powerful fame is. One day at a private event, one of the richest guys in Texas told me, "George, you got something I want." I sat there looking at him, thinking like, *What this brother want from me? He want my wife? I mean, what could I have that he wants?* He said, "I want to be famous." And he's a billionaire. I never forgot that in my life. It says a lot. After that I started looking at all of these billionaires and how they were all on television, started being in movies. Being rich ain't enough. As a young fella, I realized being rich ain't it; it's not what people make it out to be. Fame was their fulfillment.

It doesn't stop with us athletes and entertainers. I see the cycle. Look at three of the richest men in the world: Elon Musk, Bill Gates, Jeff Bezos. All chased some type of fame to go with their wealth, all lost their families. Got everything in the world except for the most precious thing our Creator's given us: the capability to build a union. We're given that information on what it takes to be happy, and it don't cost anything. Just time together. That's the only investment. It don't take money, it don't take fame. Just the giving of yourself to someone else. Yet we get distracted, we get molded by how the rich and famous are living, and we think that's how we're supposed to live. And it hardly ever works out.

Some may say or ask that me going through what I had to go through being a famous athlete put me in position to prepare my kids and set them up to deal with and avoid it. Well, that's hard to say for me because I was thrust into that world. From my experience and the understanding I have now, I would have done something else. I would have tried to have just as much success to take care of my family but not at this expense. Now I might not've gained fame or be top 75, top 50, but I think with the drive I had to be successful, I could have used that for something else. Because in the end it still comes down to family. Maybe I could have done a better job if I didn't have these distractions that come along with being a pro. There's a lot of pitfalls, a lot of holes, traps that you don't see. A lot of temptation. And temptation never takes a vacation. Especially in that NBA world. I might not've had to deal with it if I was an electrician, if I became a master plumber. Those are still good professions, still allow you to take care of your family, your wife. You could possibly have a different kind of acclaim if that's what you desire. Every rich man—and I don't care how rich he is or what he's doing—is gonna build a house that has a toilet in it. And if that son of a gun stops once, he's calling a plumber. And if I'm a master plumber and I do what I do better than almost everyone, he's going to pass the word around. *Call George. He'll get it unplugged.*

Success in this system where you have a good job and make good money, where you can take care of your family when so many others are struggling, ain't enough. Most celebrities and famous athletes have more problems than regular people. But it's alluring because all you see is the outside.

Not the ugly truth that's going on on the inside. People've walked up to me and said, "George, man I wish I was a pro ballplayer like you" or "George, I loved you man. I watched you play and all that."

But they loved me for what they saw me doing on the court, but after I got off that floor, if they followed me, they would've been like, "Oh, wait a minute!" People have their own understanding of someone being special because of what that human being can do at a particular job especially when that job brings that person fame. But they know nothing about that human being or who that human being is as a person. If they did their own research just to find out how some of these great ones, whose lives they loved, turned out, it'd be bad. That's what we don't look at. That's what we choose to ignore.

Now that I'm older, I have a better perspective on things. And once I fell in love with Joyce and we got married and had our children, that became our gift. And I gotta be able to take care of that gift. I've always had that sense of understanding. I'm just one of those guys who has been fortunate enough to play professional sports. But I know a lot of other guys who've been fortunate enough to play as well, but it didn't turn out the same. They lost everything that meant the most to them. They just didn't recognize that because they were so distracted by being in that world.

Shaquille O'Neal spoke about it on *The Pivot* podcast with those brothas Ryan Clark, Fred Taylor, and Channing Crowder. He talked real honestly about his divorces. He talked about how it haunts him and how he regrets some of the things he did that affected his family. I feel for Shaq because most people are chasing that dream that he got. But he's reaching out and saying: "Look you all: I got this big, 70,000 square-foot house, and it's quiet with no voices, no one in it."

It's scary. It's like King Solomon, who had it all. And when God spoke to him and said, "What can I give you?"

Solomon said, "Give me wisdom! All I want is wisdom."

And God told Solomon: "Since you have asked for this and not for long life or wealth for yourself, nor have asked for the death of your enemies but for discernment in administering justice, I will do what you have asked. I will give you a wise and discerning heart, so that there will never have been anyone like you, nor will there ever be." All Solomon wanted to be able to do was deal with things and take care of people. He was crying out for it, and that's what Shaq was doing. It's hard growing up in that world, where you can have anything that you want, you can buy anything you want, you can go anywhere you want. And whether you know it or not, you don't want to go anywhere by yourself. If you pay attention to what Shaq says, all he talks about is his stepfather. That shows you right there how important family is to him. He had to be hurting for a long time. He put on a good facade, but sooner or later, that human is going to come out of you. To be able to hear Shaq say what he said about that part of his life, I'm proud of him. That's why I love him.

Consciousness and choice are very important in our lives. We were created to have choice, to know right from wrong. It's a corrupt system that we're up against, and you can tell just based on something as simple as the education and both how and what they teach us. The educational system doesn't teach you the essentials. It doesn't teach you how to deal with the world you are about to be a part of. It teaches you how to depend on somebody. And my belief is if you are going to have to depend on somebody, then you need to depend on God himself. People don't have hope today, and that relationship and understanding of God is where hope comes from. The world is getting worse and worse, the system more corrupt and corrupt, none of it is getting better, and it's not getting better because it's in the hands of man, and man can't guide his own stuff. He's incapable. The more I study, the more I see that it's hard for man to help himself and help others based on how he set up the cruel world we all live in. No natural affection. That's what a lot of us in this system don't have. No room for resolution. We are already living in those kind of times where there's no natural affection or compassion for the next person. This system treats people all over the world the same way—and it's not loving. Now we people have that love for ourselves and mostly for one another, but the ones running this system are the ones who want to keep the people in bondage and under some sort of control. We love each other, but it ain't easy. Not the way they have it set up for us to live, especially when you don't have some kind of spiritual foundation to fight.

I can't help but say it because we are molded by a system that tears us down. It's a dog-eat-dog world, a system designed to make your life miserable. Some are fortunate, and most are not. That makes it tough. The ones of us who did make it, it took a lot out of us. People dream about doing what we did. We're living in a society and a system and a world where people shape their whole lives to be a part of what we do. They look at us and they idolize us in ways that are dangerous to our own well-being and mental health. And to reach the heights that some of us reach—right now in our profession there's only 75 of us—I promise if you ask each one of them, they'll all say: "I lost something to get this 75 tag on me. Something is going to happen to you." Hopefully, hopefully, it's something that you can recover from. So, again, I ask: is it worth it?

CHAPTER FIFTEEN

SUPERSTAR

One thing I could do is finger roll.

I was the sidekick. The Nike commercial was built for David Robinson. They just asked me to come along with him. We were just sitting down in the barbershop in Oakland, California, on the set in the middle of 1994. The sun was out, and they're all talking, I had the old ABA ball in my hands, and Tim Hardaway just said, "Hey, Ice, talk about that poster...where you had that jumpsuit on, 1977 butterfly collar. You walk outside in San Antonio with that on now, you'll burn up." We all started laughing. Then he said, "Tell us about that finger roll from the free-throw line."

And I just said, "That was my patented shot right there because the one thing I could do is finger roll." It just came out naturally, wasn't scripted. They all *burst* out laughing. It ended up not only making it in the commercial, but also *making* the commercial. That took it to another level. I had no idea it was going to have that type of impact, never expected it. I don't think anyone did honestly. I was just being me. And if you watch it, you'll see how I said it so innocently. People are still saying it today. But what I really liked about that commercial was that it wasn't for me. Even though they ended up building the commercial around me, the commercial itself was for someone else, and that's what I enjoyed about it the most. That's what was beautiful.

Before 1988 Nike wasn't big on using television commercials for advertising. Most of their promotion of shoes and stuff came through things like magazine ads and posters of John McEnroe. I remember all of the running posters like the one with runners laying on the ground after the Battle of Atlanta that ended up being in the movie *St. Elmo's Fire*. I also remember all of the ones with us basketball players: the original "Supreme Court" poster with 17 of us in judges robes, which I think we shot during one of The Pro Club vacations, the Moses Malone poster, and, of course, the ICEMAN poster. We did a Jam Session one with about 25 of us on an outside court like we were playing pick-up ball. Calvin Murphy was on the drums. Nike had a real cool one of Paul Westphal leaving the court on some street shooting a basketball in the air.

Things changed after that. I was told that Phil Knight had suggested to Dan Wieden and David Kennedy that they start an advertising agency, which we know now became Wieden + Kennedy, and that pretty much changed Nike into an advertising company. And the direction Nike seemed to be going wasn't posters anymore. They started getting into doing television commercials. And after the "Bo Knows" commercials and all of the Michael Jordan commercials, they started doing basketball commercials for the other Nike athletes.

I heard that in the beginning there was hesitation about me being in the first barbershop commercials because at the time Nike wanted them to be all about the younger guys like Chris Webber, Alonzo Mourning, Dennis Rodman, Robinson, and Hardaway. All of the current players. But the guys who created the concept for the commercials figured that it was a barbershop, and all barbershops have the older guys in there hanging out with the younger guys. So one of them suggested Artis Gilmore. And the other guy said, "Well, if we're using Gilmore, then we gotta add Gervin." The one guy who wanted Gilmore for the commercial wasn't a fan of me at the time, and Nike was still trying to make the commercials all about the young fellas. But somehow the creators of the commercials convinced them to get Gilmore and me in there.

All of the commercials we did from there on were just natural. All post-retirement. It seemed like Mark Thomashow was just finding ways to put me in Nike commercials. After I was in that barbershop commercial, he had me in the Little Penny Super Bowl party commercial where I was making gumbo. They had me in the LeBron James commercial, where I was sitting front row next to Rich Paul before he was James' agent. He was just one of his best friends then. Blake Wesley; who now plays for the San Antonio Spurs but was maybe four or five years old at the time; Damon Wayans; and the Sacramento Kings ownership group of the Maloof brothers (because the commercial was based around James' first NBA game and the Kings happened to be the team he played against); Detroit Lions wide receiver Calvin Johnson were all in there. I was even in two different Kevin Durant commercials. I've been told that I've had a better run as far as cameos than any other person in Nike's history.

I always had an understanding of the power of marketing and advertising, but I never looked at myself as a pitchman. I never considered being that guy. I'm really not a me-me-me type of person. But it got so big ABC wanted to do—and we actually shot—a pilot for a TV show called *Southern Fried Ice*. And as much as I never wanted to be that guy, I was that guy at one time. Once I sat down and was able to figure out everything that was going on around me at that time, I realized I was the centerpiece. I did so many things strictly out of passion. But in hindsight I think if I'd been more on the business side of the things, I probably could have been that pitchman to the point that today I still could be doing it.

But by the time those things started happening, especially with Nike and Wieden + Kennedy, Knight was trying to get his product out so that everyone could wear it. He was busy. He was building the brand on the corporate level; he was CEO. He'd reached a point where he was able to put others in place to do what he used to do so that now he could really concentrate on running a company. And those people who he put in place weren't as familiar with me as he was. If Knight had of been the one to keep pushing it and looking for advertising opportunities, I know I probably still would have been the pitchman. But timing plays a role in everything. Thomashow always says, "If Nike had been in television advertising 10 years earlier. George, you would have been its featured guy."

We did do a whole cooking show series of commercials. Me and Elise Neal. It was called "The Iceman Cooketh." Stacy Wall created them. Their whole idea was to take two Nike players in every city and highlight them by doing commercials about them. I think we did maybe 30 commercials. At this point it had probably been about four years since I'd retired. I remember Thomashow not thinking I would do the commercials. He showed me the idea they had for the campaign, and I didn't immediately respond. I ended up calling him back from the golf course. "Hey, Mark, saw the campaign," I said before not saying anything for a while after that. I was messing with him. Then after a long, long pause, I said, "You know I love it!" I started laughing and then hung up. We did those commercials for two years.

On one commercial for New York Knicks star Darrell Walker, the food we were basing the commercial around was cinnamon rolls. And during a break in this one, there was an Iceman Cooketh Nerf hoop about 15 feet away from where they had me. Wall said, “Hey, George, since this is about this player’s jump shot, while you’re saying your lines, just see if you can shoot one of the cinnamon rolls into the hoop over there.” These were real cinnamon rolls—sticky and all of that—plus he’s asking me to do this while looking into the camera. So I looked into the camera and I said my lines and I just turned and started shooting the rolls. In one take I drained 18 of ’em.

We had fun. I shot one in Los Angeles with Diddy, which The Rock was supposed to be in. I sat in on LeBron James’ first Nike commercial in the church, the one where Bernie Mac was the preacher. And that was great because Dr. J, Jerry West, and Malone were in it, too. Even had the comedian Joe Torry in some of the commercials we did. I know he was definitely in the first barbershop commercial because you can hear him at the very end. And to bring this full circle, the song they used in that first commercial was from the movie *Superfly*. That just goes to back what I was saying about growing up and what was cool.

I never thought about the role the commercials played in people connecting with me and connecting with my personality. Never thought while we were doing them how they seemed to touch people. Somehow it all aligned. But this was when I knew it was too much for me: around 1995 Reggie Theus had an NBC Saturday morning show called *Hang Time*, where he played a high school basketball coach. I interviewed for that in the late 1990s because Theus was leaving the show. I got in front of all the executives, the producers, the showrunners, the ones who were in control—and it scared me. That was the first time I'd ever really seen what I consider darkness in my adult life. I went in the room to do my read, and there were eight men and women dressed in black. It terrified me. Not specifically them, but the feeling inside of that room. I wasn't ready for that, so I didn't read well. Nothing went well. Before I went in there, everyone told me from a preparation standpoint, "You got it." I knew the script word for word. I knew everything down to the punctuation of every word I had to read and every movement they wanted in that scene for the character. That's how natural and prepared I was. But when I went into that room and saw and felt that atmosphere, I lost it all. I was done.

That's when I knew that Hollywood game, that life, it wasn't made for me. That angel that looked over me back in high school, I ran into that angel again that day. This whole thing took place on the Universal Studios lot in California. One of the executive producers walked up right before the read and said to me, "You ready, Ice?"

"Yes sir," I replied, because I was. Then he took me back in that room.

I was good at it, and acting came easy to me. I read scripts with veteran actors, some I still see on TV today, and they'd sit and look at each other because they thought I was new, and instead I'd impress them. They'd tell me, "Ice, what you got, people go to school for." So I knew that could have been my new game. I would have made $30,000 an episode, and there were 26 episodes a season. Somehow that angel knew had I continued down that road, that my soul may have gone with it. That angel saved me. That's the only thing that makes sense to me because that same angel that's been with me this whole time knew that wasn't my world, knew I wasn't supposed to be there.

CHAPTER SIXTEEN

RINGS

My real trophy is people.

With me being one of the ones who's been a part of this from the beginning to see how the franchise has grown, when the San Antonio Spurs got that first ring, I remember that feeling was real special. I had to keep reminding people that the teams I was on had won some divisional titles, got some banners up there, too. We just didn't win it all. But this feeling was different. And I'd still been with the organization since I retired. I was there when they got David Robinson. Now, it took him a few years to get him one. He had to get someone else—and that somebody happened to be Tim Duncan—to get that first one. Then they got Tony Parker, then they got Manu Ginobili. They built a solid basketball team. Seeing the building of that was incredible to me. But to be at that first celebration at the Alamodome was amazing. When Robinson got up there at that celebration to speak, he was asked a question: "David, what do you want to be remembered like after all of this is over?"

He answered: "I want to be remembered like George Gervin!" He said that in front of 50,000 people. That right there tells you how I felt when we won that first ring.

It's so easy for people to forget that we were a winning franchise before the Spurs won that first championship. And it wasn't just me. We had some unbelievable teams in our era. I had some bad boys with me in San Antonio during my career. We had enough. We just didn't do enough. From 1982 to 1988 the San Antonio Spurs had to play the Los Angeles Lakers in the Western Conference playoffs. During that time our record against Magic Johnson and them was 2–14. They swept us in three of the four series. So when we faced them again in 1995 in the Western Conference Semifinals, it was a big deal for the franchise. The next time we saw them in the playoffs was four years later, and we had Duncan then. Once we swept them in those Western Conference Semifinals in 1999, we knew we had a chance to win it all.

It all goes back to what I was saying about ownership of the organization. Once they got going, they had people who were smart enough to bring in people who gave them a chance to win it all. And that started when they went after Robinson. They were smart and patient because Robinson sat out two years due to his Naval Academy commitment. But the Spurs waited on him. Got Larry Brown to come in as head coach, got Terry Cummings from the Milwaukee Bucks, drafted Sean Elliott. They went from having the worst record in franchise history with 20 wins to the next year, when Robinson finally came, to winning 56 games. One of the best one-season turnarounds in the history of the NBA. And at that time Red McCombs had taken over as primary owner. Then things fell into place. They get Duncan, then they got two international players, Parker and Ginobili, with something to prove. And then they get a coach, Gregg Popovich, who came in with a system. Military background. And he got the talent around him who he felt could fit that system. And then they started rollin'. Fortunately for Pop he had guys who were young enough to keep building off that system. And they began winning championships every other year for the five years between 2003 and 2007. That's pretty big.

The most important part of this game you can learn or be taught is how to work and play with others. Now you're always going to have a few who stand out individually, but you learn the only way any team is going to be able to win a championship is to play the game the way it was designed: as a team. A lot of success comes from that formula. That's what I love about Pop. Guys buy into his formula. He has a system. And he implemented that system and allowed everyone to share in it. Duncan, Robinson, Ginobili, Bruce Bowen, Parker, and Avery Johnson, they all shared in it. And they were all with Pop and his system for so long and did it so well that it changed lives.

People always ask me, especially after the franchise won all of those championships, "George, who is the greatest Spur?"

This is the analogy I give them: "Say the Spurs are a tree. I'm the roots of the tree, and then David Robinson is the trunk of the tree, and Tim Duncan is the branches, leaves, and flowers."

Now I'm not going to try to compare myself to Duncan or Robinson. I'll let people make their own comparisons. But I do know a tree can't grow without roots; that's the foundation. And without that foundation, it can't have a trunk, and without a trunk, it can't get any branches, flowers, or leaves. And I say this with nothing but love for Duncan and Robinson and what they did, but I know who I am to the franchise. So how can I not feel good about what the Spurs were able to do and my part in it if I look at it with an open heart and open eyes?

I'm comfortable with not winning a championship while I was playing because of the respect we got around the league. They respected the Spurs. Every team we played, they knew they had to come with it. It was more than just me, and everyone in the league knew it. Yes, I was the key guy, but there were a bunch of other keys there, too, that teams had to contain. Any of them on any or every given night could go off. Larry Kenon could go off and give you

30 points and 20 rebounds. He was James Worthy—before James Worthy.

But pressure to be the first ABA team to win an NBA championship while I was playing? Naw, we didn't carry that pressure. Opportunity? Yes, we gave ourselves that. Western Conference Finals twice, Eastern Conference Finals once, a Game Seven Western Conference Semifinals loss to the Houston Rockets, five division titles. We gave ourselves a chance.

I kept this game as a game. It wasn't life. It was my job, but it was still a game. I never let it control my life and I didn't play it to win at all costs. I never looked at it like all or nothing. I looked at it as human beings playing a kids' game and getting paid for it. Somebody is going to win. Most are going to lose. Relationships that came from the game, those meant everything to me, not the wins or loses. Throughout my young life to my old life to now, it's always been that way. And as people who've gotten to know me—the people who did my documentary, who are now telling the story of my life—have found out I touched some people's lives. And that's what I'd like to be known for. I don't wanna be known as someone who won five championships or four scoring titles. My job was to play ball, try to win games, try to win championships, entertain, and have an opportunity to see the world and meet people. All of that came true for me. And I'm proud of it, so proud that I have that. Because you see guys who have championships and celebrated a lot of winning, and that's only one aspect of the game. One aspect of why you are supposed to play and what you are supposed to get out of the game. The most beautiful part we all have at our disposal as players is when it's all over we can look back and ask: where am I at in life? What do I have in my life? And for me, if I looked back and didn't have the relationships that I have, then I got nothing. So take those trophies and those rings; you all can have 'em. My real trophy is people.

* * *

Michael Jordan and Scottie Pippen, I can't believe where they're at. With all of the success they had together, it hurts me to see that. Kinda like it was with Shaquille O'Neal and Kobe Bryant. They dominated the game. Then, to see how things got, to see what came out of it, makes you wonder if they really appreciated each other. Because it turned so ugly. Bryant and Shaq were able to settle their differences before Bryant passed away, which was great. But all of that time, they spent kind of sparring despite all they accomplished. I mean, it bothers me because I'm a relationship guy. If that's the makeup of a champion, I'm glad I didn't win it all.

Any marriage—your personal marriage or your basketball marriage—is tough. As players we're with each other more than we are with our wives and families sometimes. And we're talking now about some of the greatest who ever played. How are they not going to be happy for each other for what they've accomplished together? How are they not complimenting each other? Unless there was a devil there all along. And all the devil does is separate. It's so ugly. I just hope and I pray that ain't true. That's what bothers me the most because I have nothing but respect for all of them for what they accomplished. Jordan and Pippen won six championships together; Shaq and Bryant won three in a row. I only played with Jordan, and that was before Pippen got there, but for them to end up being like this? C'mon. I look at their careers and I look at mine, and for me to have the kind of relationships with the guys who I've played with, I'm better off without the ring. Because I still got a lotta love for my guys. And they still got love for me. Because when it's all said and done, it's just us anyway.

We watched it with Kevin Garnett and Ray Allen and Paul Pierce. We watched it with Kyrie Irving and LeBron James. Dr. J and I laugh about our time to this day. He'll tell anybody, "Ice was my rookie." And he'll see me and be like, "Hey, rookie, go get me some donuts."

And I'm like, "Where you want me to go get 'em? What time you want 'em?" If people say I was Doc's rookie, I'm proud to have that title. Now I know Dr. J and I didn't spend the same amount of time together and go through all of the things that a lot of these other players had to go through as teammates in order to win a championship, but ours is a great relationshp. To me that has to mean something. We're both in our 70s and we're still just as close. And to me no ring's worth losing that.

It just makes me sad, and I pray that these brothas find a way to forgive each other and hug each other again and recognize just what they were able to do as teammates because the game was designed for us to be teammates first and then win. For Jordan and Pippen, that would be the greatest joy. And a lot of that stuff will come out of them with just a hug. Magic Johnson and Isiah Thomas, they weren't even teammates, but look at how close they were, look at how driven they both were to get those rings, look at how they got torn apart from one another, and look at how it all came out and got better with one another once they hugged. But Magic and Larry Bird were different. They battled, won rings against one another, but the love they have for one another stayed undefeated. As much as the world tried to play that narrative: Black vs. White, East Coast vs. West Coast, Celtics vs. Lakers, Los Angeles vs. Boston, Bird and Magic showed that they're bigger that that. Their relationship was bigger than that. And if they had let that negative narrative work, it could have really had an impact on younger people coming up. But they didn't fall for it. I love that about both of them.

They weren't selfish. That's the answer. To me, that's always what it comes down to. It's the power of what being selfish can do. And what creates selfishness? Pride, ego, boastfulness, divisiveness, all of the ugly things. That means those players had all of those ugly things floating around, and for them to end up like they did when it comes to their relationships with one another, it comes back to relationships. We don't put enough value on them. The truth is if you don't have someone to love and someone to love you, you're lost. I don't care how much money or fame or whatever you got or how many Super Bowls or Academy Awards you've won, if you don't have those little necessities of life—those relationships, those people—it gets you nowhere.

I'm really at peace with myself, where I'm at with the career I had, with the people I was able to play with, and the things that we did together while having to play that game for a living. Because I loved it and I loved what came from it—not just what I got out of it. A lot of men have shown us after their careers are over that their drive and understanding of what they did consumed them. Now why would I do that? I ain't gotta win at all costs. If I did, who would I have been serving? I play inside the rules, I try every time on that court to do my best to win, and if I don't, I'm going home. Still intact. Think about it: the guy who will win at all costs got issues, and it ain't good.

Every player I ever played with or against, I can walk up to them today and say, "Wassup, you got 40 on me."

And they say, "Ice, you know you the one who got 40 on me." Then we laugh about it. Nothing's greater to me in this game than to be able to do that.

Ecclesiastes 9:11 is one of my favorite passages in scripture and it tells us plain and simple: "Time and unforeseen occurrences can befall all of us." People don't look at that as reality. So to be able to live that basketball afterlife where me and the guy I either played against or played with still have a good relationship, when we see each other are both healthy, we both still have good or decent lifestyles, and we still caring about the ones who don't have much, that's everything.

I was like that with the Spurs owners, too. I went to go see Angelo Drossos at his house before he died. He didn't even know me. I went with Bob Bass. I'm close with Angelo's son, John, who lives in Dallas. And Angelo's wife, Lillie, is still alive. She took me into his room. It was sad to see him like that. We lost Angelo. Then Red McCombs was like that. I was trying to get him included in the book, but he's too far gone before passing away in February of 2023. They were good to me, Drossos and McCombs. I think I'm still working for the Spurs because of McCombs. I'm still in the front office for them. So that tells you not just how I feel about them, but also how they feel about me. It goes all the way back to the beginning.

CHAPTER SEVENTEEN

GOLF

What could have been…

Golf is one of the greatest games man can play. And we like to play games; that's what man does. That's why golf is so addictive. It's that powerful. It's frustrating if you don't keep it recreational, it's time-consuming, it's a game you can't beat, it reveals character, it's so difficult it makes you want to cheat, it's a challenge that no man will defeat or perfect or ever conquer.

I play. When I say play, I mean I can play. I gotta single-digit handicap. I practice all of the time. The same with basketball: I put the work in. I applied those same principles, so I'm proud of my golf game. It would be hard for a weekend golfer to beat me because they can't put the time in that I have. They're working all week whereas I'm practicing and playing every day, chipping, putting. I'm working on those certain aspects of the game that you have to have confidence in for you to be good at it: driving the ball, studying the greens, knowing how to get out of the sand traps, getting that feel on my putts, keeping composure. Composure is big in golf. A lot of people get mad and throw their clubs. They're not that good anyway, but they still throw their clubs. It's a game of misses, and you gonna miss—a lot! But it's all about how can you recover from a miss. It plays with your mind; it can mentally break you if you let it. And it takes time to master that part of the game, the mental part. That's what separates the greats from everyone else. The great ones are able to figure it out.

* * *

I used to work at Dr. Robert Sims' house on Strathmoor Street off Woodward Avenue and Seven Mile in Detroit when I was a kid. That's how I met Marvin Gaye. It goes back that far. He lived around the corner from Dr. Sims. His life story is unbelievable. Dr. Sims knows everybody, and everybody knows him. But at the same time, he's not as well-known as he should be. He's like Clarence Avant; he's the other Black Godfather. And when he sits in that chair like he did in my documentary, he looks just like The Godfather. Like The Don. Sims not only worked for General Motors for all of those years, but he was also a doctor for the Public School League in Detroit, had his own practice, and everything. And Doc Sims was the one who introduced me to golf when I was young, but I wasn't ready for it. And now I can't get off the course. Doc Sims was a big-time golfer, an amateur golfer but still big time. He worked at it. I mean, he practiced all of the time. And these were the things I didn't see, but I learned about him and golf over time. About his dedication to the game. He used to let me caddy for him at mid-regional tournaments in the Michigan area. They played 36 holes a day. So I carried his bags. He was teaching me the game as I was carrying his bags. But I wasn't paying that much attention to what he was telling me or the game at the time. I was around 14 or 15 years old and all I was thinking about was when is this going to end. Man, 36 holes, I was worn out. He'd give me a little money for helping him out, and then I didn't want to do it anymore. It was a done deal for me. But it wasn't until later that I realized he really wasn't doing it because he needed me to caddy. He was slowly introducing me to the game because I think he knew how important golf could be after my retirement. He was prepping me. It was almost like he was working on my retirement plan before I even had a career because it's after retirement where I feel we athletes start to run into tough times. He knew I was going to need something else in my life besides basketball.

Doc Sims has been into golf all of his life. He actually spearheaded the Tiger Woods Foundation. He knew Earl Woods, Tiger's dad, through the military. They served in the army together. And because of Doc Sims, I got to see Tiger play as a kid. Before most people. Got to know his dad, Earl. Doc Sims used to fund Tiger's amateur career. He knew with Tiger's potential how important it was back then for Tiger to get as much exposure as possible. He knew Tiger needed to be able to go off and play in these tournaments all over the country to get seen. So Doc Sims and his leadership group were the ones who helped finance the early stages of Earl and Tiger's journey and he got to be a part of their lives in Tiger's early days. They made sure Tiger got on those professional golf courses like the Riviera Country Club in Palisades, California, and private, ritzy places—where we, Black folks, were allowed to cook the food but not get on the course—like the Alamo Country Club in Texas before he turned professional. That was a big part of it because if you don't play on these types of golf courses it's going to be tough when you have to play on them and you aren't used to those conditions or courses. That's what Doc Sims and his partners believed in.

He and his team also had Earl and Tiger go to inner-city golf courses to do clinics and camps because Doc Sims also knew how important that type of exposure was going to be for them. He did that for Tiger and Earl for years until IMG came in and took over. People of color really didn't start playing golf at a high level at a more noticeable rate until Tiger got into the game. He changed the game. And this is a part of Tiger's story that isn't talked about, and Doc Sims is at the center of it. The story itself is so big and it becomes a part of my story because of what Doc Sims has done for me. The stories connect.

In my mind I was introduced to this game by a pioneer. That's what Doc Sims is: a pioneer in this game. That's part of the reason it's important to me. I didn't understand it when

I was young and I didn't really start playing until I retired. Just like Doc Sims figured I would. And I always go back to the man who put this game in my life. Doc Sims and Bill Dickey, another pioneer who's one of Doc Sims' partners, has the Bill Dickey Scholarship Association and the Bill Dickey Invitational Junior Golf Tournament that help create opportunities for young golfers of color to compete in golf and get a foot in to the business world. I watched them build a foundation these young Black and Brown babies could stand on. A lot of young African American golfers got scholarships from Sims and Dickey, and some got on the PGA Tour coming through their organizations. Even as popular as the game is today, a lot of our kids still don't have the access and exposure. I always wonder how just being exposed to golf at such an early age, coming from where I come from and what I had to go through, translated into what it has become in my life now.

Had I taken a liking to golf early when Doc Sims was laying the groundwork on me, I really don't know what could have been. Especially playing the role he did in Tiger's early career and especially knowing the work I put into things. I just think about what I know about myself. One thing I know about life is you get better when you put in the work and I had that habit of putting in the work. If golf had been my calling, I know I would've put in the work if I'd have fallen in love with it. I was in love with basketball so I did all of the things it took to get better. If I had the same mind-set in golf, I honestly think I could have gotten to the next level. I mean, I had the mind-set and mentality that plays into my ability to execute, and you can tell how proficient I was at that by looking analytically at my professional basketball career. Analytically, I was good, one of the best. That means I was good statistically, and that comes from being mentally locked in and being efficient and believing—all the things you need to be either really good or great at golf.

So yes, I think I could have been successful. Definitely could have made a career out of it and been on the PGA tour. Now could I have been a champion? A Tiger, Arnold Palmer, Lee Trevino, and all of that? I don't know. I don't even allow myself to think like that. I'm not that gullible. And I love me, but I'm going to be fair to myself.

People get on me for having a reputation for not playing defense during my basketball career. I always wondered where they got that from. Also, I'm not sure if they mean *couldn't* or *didn't* play defense, but I think they mean couldn't. Even my guys today, they always say when we're on the golf course, "Well, Ice, you know you really weren't known for your defense."

And I always have to come up with my own answer: "They ain't pay me to play D. They paid guys to guard me." That shuts them up for a while.

But that whole thing hurts my feelings a bit. And on the golf course with them, it's worse. "Yeah, we gonna get you on this putt, Ice. We gonna make you play defense because you ain't known for defense."

So I remind them, "Yeah, but I'm known for putting the ball in the hole. And that applies out here on these courses the same way it did on those courts."

I'm more amazed at what professional golfers can do than I am what professional basketball players can do. In golf it's just you. You and the ball and the clubs. To me that takes more concentration, takes more confidence to play, and the mental aspect of the game weighs on you more. You have to concentrate all of the time. You don't get a timeout in golf. The timeout is when you miss the cut or the round is over. You don't get subbed out either. And under trials and tribulations in sports, we athletes all think differently. The great ones again, they are the ones who are able to figure it out. If you gotta two-foot putt to win a tournament, most players, even the pros, their hands start shaking. They get the yips. And I know because I developed the yips to the point that I was actually nervous to make a two- or three-foot putt. It's a mental block. So I had to change the way I putted. Now I don't have the yips anymore because I made the change. This is something I never had playing basketball. But in golf there's something all of the time because you are always chasing it.

Basketball is a game of reaction; golf is a game of challenge. And life's been a challenge my whole life.

It's the void filler for me. I had a basketball career for almost 40 years from the time I picked up a ball and started playing every day, I hadn't found anything to fill that void. Golf did that for me just by the way the game is designed. You play against the courses not against the person. You move that ball around the course because it's a game of character. It has the power to expose who you really are because it's so hard it makes you want to cheat, because it forces you to see how good you can get at the game by playing by the rules, because you can play with anybody of any age. That's the beauty of it.

Sometimes I'm good; sometimes I'm awful. But my character never changes. As hard as the game is, I never let it pull me out of who I am. What golf over the years has made me learn about myself is that I'd go into business with me. Just based on what the game says about one's character. People say it's just a game. Yeah, but it reveals so much. I've played with guys who cheat, and that tells me that's bad character. It tells you something about yourself. I know I ain't perfect. I done rolled my ball a few times when I shouldn't have, but I prefer and almost always play the game the way it is designed. Can you play 18 holes the right way? That's tough to do. But it's shown me that winning ain't more valuable than the game, shown me through that approach that I have values.

CHAPTER EIGHTEEN

THE CIRCLE

Everyone can't work life out by themselves.

I love life and then I love people. That's a part of who created us. That's what He does. He loves life and He loved creation and He created us all. Sometimes you don't like some of the folks that we run into over the course of life, and that's not always easy to deal with. I kept my circle small. Throughout my life I had a circle that I kept for a long time, and very few got into it. I'm fortunate. I *know* the people in my circle. James Morgan or "Bull," who I went to elementary school, middle school, high school, and college with, is in it, and so is Gary Tyson, who played point guard with me in high school and college. Jerry Lee and his family. Craig Simpson and Ralph Simpson. Freeman Sparks, my former high school basketball teammate. Coach Willie Merriweather. Dr. Robert Sims. Ain't very many more.

It's either grade school, high school, or college folks. That's by design. When you come up and become a young pro like I did, you wonder early: *why does this person want to be around me?* I already knew all of my other guys, I came up with them, they helped me get there. I know these guys love me because they've been through tribulations with me. To some people a friend to them is someone they might socialize with sometimes. For me a friend is deeper than that. You gotta understand. We live unfortunately in a different world. I saw Derek Jeter talk about that in his documentary, *The Captain*. We are in a world full of wolves dressed in sheep's clothing. It's a different world there. They drip blood at the mouth, but when they come up to you, it's all wiped off. But at the same time, they're ready to cut your neck off, get whatever they can from you and move on, and get the next one.

I can't say that I've come up with someone outside of my original circle who I've actually let in later on in life. You find out that you don't need 'em. In high school we came up in what they'd now call a gang. We grew up in a time and an atmosphere where there were a bunch of us and all we had was each other. Somebody do something to one of us, and somebody else gonna get it. As you get out of high school, that whole thing kinda busts up. Everyone starts goin' their own way.

In many ways I'm almost an introvert. I never really let anyone penetrate that circle. The people in my circle never had any trust issues. They'd been there to help build my game, my confidence, my self-esteem and always had my best interest in their hearts. I owed a lot to them. All of them. And I never felt that I really needed anything more in life. We got almost 50, some 60 years together. That's a lifetime. If you can hold on to those type of people in your life, why would you need anything else?

At the same time, people will be people, and there are times in life where we are all reminded of that. For my wife Joyce and

I one of those times was in 1989 when this property company in Washington, who we were in partnership with for an apartment complex in Tacoma, Washington, tried to sue us. The complex was one of my big investments after my career was over, and we ended up filing bankruptcy on the property. The case was *Gervin v. Cadles of Grassy Meadows*, a loan obligation case that started out in the lower courts, which ended up becoming a statute case cited in the Supreme Court. The case went on for years. It didn't end until 2005. I remember the judge saying, "Time ran out! Game over! Gervin wins!" Almost like an announcer at a basketball game. He actually wrote that in the brief.

We fought them and beat them. Basically, Grassy Meadows was found guilty of being in contempt of "violating our discharge injunction." That's how the court papers put it. It really became Joyce's case because she ended up filing a suit against Cadles for emotional distress during the process, and the courts decided that emotional damage was inflicted on Joyce and sided with her. The whole experience was a reminder for us about the other side of humans and human behavior. Like everything else you got people who are greedy. I've had a few difficult times in my life publicly and left myself open for people to maybe take advantage. Some people call them "opportunists." Sort of like Satan did to Jesus when he was out in the wilderness for 40 days and he was hungry and weak, felt he could take advantage of Him.

But one of the things I love most is that these brothas in our circle never really tried to tell me what to do. Instead, they were always there right with me trying to help me work things out. It's more than just a support system. People, who love you, don't tell you what to do. When people love you, they make you ask yourself the questions that need to be asked. And they do it in a loving way. Because when you are down on yourself, it's fragile. You're sensitive. That's when you lose relationships. My guys know how to deal with me in a way that I wouldn't blow up on them, or they wouldn't blow up on me. We wouldn't lose or jeopardize our friendship. Everyone doesn't have those kinds of relationships. Our circle has lost some of them, but the core of us are still here, and we're rare. And we know how rare we are to each other.

I've never thought about life without them because I've always had them. I've never been anywhere in my life really without them. I know a lot of people can't say that. A lot of people haven't had what I have with these types of friendships and relationships. A lot of people are on that island by themselves. And that's tough. No one to talk to, no one to tell you the truth. That feedback, the other voice beside your own, that's important for growth. And to have guys and family, sisters and brothers, my wife and kids, who are going to be there and have been there for me in those moments—no matter what—means the world.

CHAPTER NINETEEN

COMMUNITY

The greatest protection we can have is to display love for others.

When I started thinking about creating my own programs after my career, I was doing work with the San Antonio Spurs providing community service for probably five, six, seven years. All NBA teams have community service programs where members of the team, players, front office, coaches, staff go out into the communities and let those communities know that it's not just about buying tickets and supporting the team. It's about contributing to the community to help different programs, especially ones that are helping kids. These programs are what got me thinking about what I could do individually because I was already doing it with the Spurs. I was already out in the community. Once I had a good understanding of how this works, I figured I'd start my own program. It wasn't about what the Spurs weren't doing; it was about my own innovation. I like to say, "An artist paints his own pictures." And I've always considered myself an artist. That's when I called my sister, Barbara, who at the time was my accountant and is now a district state representative for Texas, and said, "Let's start creating."

This was about me being thankful about what the Spurs organization were already doing. As time grew and as the franchise grew, I really believe they realized how important community service really was to the franchise. And as they grew, they also believed in their ability to provide different services to those communities. I've always been a part of that. Because of that I'd probably been to every elementary school, middle school, and high school in the city of San Antonio and Bexar County, Texas, due to my relationship with the Spurs. The Coyote mascot and I used to go everywhere together. It's funny that we were a duo. We went into these schools and were a part of their Read to Achieve programs and all of those types of programs that the school's themselves sponsored. When the schools needed someone from the Spurs to come out and help promote their programs, we'd show up. By the time 1991 came around, I'd been been back from Baki Manresa in Spain, where I played internationally, and fully retired from the game and I had a clear idea. Through my sister's help, we started the George Gervin Youth Center. I like saying, "It's George's name and Barbara's brain that made this happen." I get you in the door; she closes it.

We started in a strip mall on Broadway Street by the airport in San Antonio in '91 with a $150,000 budget. At the time San Antone was really just starting to grow, so we were kind of getting in on the ground floor. Once the youth center got going and the city began to grow, we grew along with it and started other different programs under that umbrella. We have George Gervin Youth Centers around San Antonio and the office building on Denver Boulevard. As time passed we went from the youth centers to charter schools. We became one of the first of 20 charter schools in the state of Texas. And this was when George W. Bush was governor. I'll never forget when Bush came to one of the games. He was there with the owner of the Spurs at that time, Peter Holt, and Holt introduced us, and Bush said, "I know who the Iceman is." And he went on to tell me how much he appreciated what I was doing in the community with our schools.

We started out at the charter schools with a dropout recovery program. San Antonio has always been either No. 1 or 2 in the nation in teen pregnancy rates and high school dropout rates. If you look back to the late 1970s to early 1980s, we had a dropout population of ninth graders in the millions across the country. We were losing our babies in this school system. As my sister says, "This city does not do well by its young people at all. Especially minorities. They don't prepare them." So we started our own to try and help fill that void, to help save some of these kids. At least here in Texas. In the beginning we got a lot of kids who were dropping out in 10th grade, but they still wanted to graduate. From there we were able to implement accelerating courses to help them not only graduate, but also graduate on time with the same class they came into high school with just at a different school.

That became pretty popular because the kids were investing in it and pushing themselves. It was almost like our schools were re-energizing them. We became an A school because of it, and A schools are considered some of the top schools in the city. In 2022 we dropped down to a B school level with an 85 rating. And mostly that had to do with the pandemic. Before the pandemic we were averaging 1,400 to 1,500 kids a year. Post-pandemic it's been around 800.

We didn't see what we were able to do; we saw what we could do. My sister took me to three different buildings. There was one on Grissom Road, which she called the "Taj Mahal." At the time this gorgeous building was just an empty doctor's office. Beautiful concrete driveway. Kept in good condition. All you had to do was move in. The next was an old abandoned medal building on St. Mary's Street. Then there was an old Pizza Hut warehouse on Sunbelt Drive. And once we got to that building and I walked down those atrium steps, I looked at Barabara and said, "This is us." That was our first school.

The vision we had for the other facilities started at the Catholic convent on the east side of the city. It was a 15-acre abandoned convent. It had beautiful buildings, but no one was taking care of them. What Barbara originally envisioned was a substance abuse program for inner-city children because most of the substance abuse programs at that time in the late 1980s or early 1990s were out in rural areas or out in the country areas where it was hard to get to if you were in the city. Those folks couldn't get out there to see their kids. That didn't work out.

In order for us to set up what we wanted, it was going to cost us $4.5 million off the top. We didn't have that; so it became an impossibility for us to do. So my sister saw an abandoned auto repair place down the road at 3030 East Commerce Street. It was a shell of a building sitting on about an acre of land that she knew she could redesign and turn into a school. My sister understands construction. I never thought that you could get a 50,000-square foot building on an acre of land, but she did. She researched it down to the soil, found out what it took to build, and went around to see what would be the best way to construct it. She went and got a contractor, and it was almost as if they created the walls first at the construction company and put the building together around the walls almost like a puzzle. It was a new way of building. I remember Barbara and the contractor walking around and discussing what the building could be. It became the George Gervin Technology Center.

And once we started building she noticed—because you couldn't really see anything around where we were building because it was really nothing but woods—that surrounding it was more land. There were 21 more acres. From that she knew we could expand. And here's the funny thing: we built ours before the Spurs built the AT&T Center, which is close by. It's actually walking distance. The difference is the county gave them $175 million to build, and we got $120,000.

Like my sister envisioned, we've been able to expand since then. We have the original George Gervin Academy on Sunbelt Drive, the George Gervin El Hombre de Heilo on Blanco Road, and the George Gervin Prep Academy in Phoenix, Arizona. Barbara and I always talk about how this all is connected to how we came up as kids. Her construction knowledge comes from us growing up and moving around to a lot of different houses. We moved all across East Detroit. We were poor, but our mom wouldn't allow us to be poor and destitute or live in squalor. Every house we lived in, we fixed up or renovated. We paneled the walls, put vinyl on the floors, we painted. Barbara jokingly called us the "YCPs," the Young Construction People.

The George Gervin Preparatory in Phoenix opened up a facility in 2012 because a friend of mine wanted me to come there to do basketball camps. And Barbara said to me, "If we do anything there, it has to be associated with education or it won't be sustainable. You can't just do basketball camps." So we went there and looked around and we finally found eight acres. Empty. Nothing on it. And in Phoenix a lot of their charter schools are operating out of warehouses, and we didn't want that for our kids. So we literally built that school from the ground up.

Part of the reason we did this was because I looked at what they weren't teaching in high schools that applied to the life these kids were going to live. We saw a lot of young people who'd lost respect for learning and who'd grown to become problematic. At the same time, these schools didn't teach these kids about taxes, how to balance a checkbook, or what happens once you become a felon. They weren't preparing them for the system we live in. That creates mental health problems for our young people because they don't have schools or learning centers in place to prevent a lot of these things we see our young people going through today.

These are real life experiences that can save people if we have educational systems in place to recognize them and deal with them. It should be just as important as math, science, social studies. It's scary that we don't have that in place in all schools. When I was in school, we did at least have trade schools. There were classes like home economics, wood shop, and electronics. All of those skillsets could help you create businesses for yourselves. You also need to understand felonies because if you become a felon you are no longer part of the system anymore; they basically crucify you. And you need to know about taxes because once you make a certain amount of money you get into a certain tax bracket and have to pay differently. These might seem like simple things, but in the long run, it's essential for young people to get educated so they can become functional parts of this society and world we are living in. And people wonder why we have so many young people with mental heath issues? Because the ones who are in charge are not making it better for the ones who are growing up to become the ones shaping our communities.

Our programs haven't been perfect, but it's been close. There was a Texas Education Agency investigation in connection with elevated military enlistment claims in 2019 that included ours and 11 other school districts. They ended up the next year ending the whole military enlistment accountability system for all graduates of Texas public high schools and other schools in the other districts in Texas' academic accountability system. Then we had to close one of our foster care homes for up to 21 days because my sister Francis, who was the CEO/superintendent, retired. At that George Gervin Basic Center, we provided temporary foster care, food, housing, health care for girls ages 12 to 17.

These initiatives were done in pieces. Only now 30 years later do we realize how large this has become. My sisters and I never thought about this as a whole campus type of deal. We didn't build it that way. We were always singularity focused on one school, one program at a time. We gradually built it to what it's become. We never took on more than we felt we could do in that moment because we wanted to do it right.

* * *

I was driving to my office at the San Antonio Spurs' facility, and the owner, Peter Holt, happened to be pulling up at the same time. He saw me and waited. Now life has its own challenges, and it's funny how those challenges are met. He said, "GG, how you doing?"

I said in kind of a low key tone, "I'm doing good, Peter. How are you?"

He said, "You know you've never asked me for anything."

I said, "Well, you all have always taken good care of me, and we have a great relationship."

Then he said, "My wife and I decided to give you a half-million dollars for your program." Just like that. I almost fell out of my car in the parking lot.

So we built a 50,000-square-foot gym with three NBA-size floors inside with that donation from Holt, his wife, and the Spurs. Everything is community-based. All of the programs. It's for people with drug issues, early pregnancy issues, runaway teenagers, low-income people, elderly folks, all community service type situations. Been doing this for 30 years. I've spent more time doing this than I did playing professional basketball. Since this whole thing started, we've built retirement homes. We felt that it'd be good to bring some of the older, retired people over to the school to work with the younger kids. We actually built one right next to the original school on Sunbelt Drive and called it the Newell Center. That's named after my grandmother. Then there's another one called the George Gervin Retirement Home for lower-income Section 202 and disabled individuals in San Antonio. In total we have three retirement homes: two in San Antonio and one in Gonzales, about 70 miles south of San Antonio.

I'm a product of programs from how my mom raised us. We were always in them. My whole life has been about programs. I came up in them as a kid. As a grown person, I went through them because of my own bad choices and now I develop them. So I know how they work. Even though I'm devout, I try not to put God in the programs. I try to stay more on the human aspect of it because everyone doesn't believe in God, and our mission first and foremost is to help people. I'm trying to help people regain their own strength and allow them to find God on their own time and at their own pace. Programs work for kids in the summertime when they don't have much to do, and if no one is creating programs for them to make money or give them a safe place to know where they are, then they'll get lost. That's a big part of the reason we started the programs. I was a product of that same existence.

At the time we began doing this, I hadn't heard of any former player doing anything like it. Jalen Rose came to me and told me that he looked at what I was doing, and that helped him decide to open his Jalen Rose Leadership Academy in our hometown of Detroit. David Robinson started his IDEA Carver Academy after I started mine. Magic Johnson opened his Bridgescape Academies around the country after we did ours. And then LeBron James recently opened his I PROMISE School in his hometown of Akron, Ohio, several years ago.

Deion Sanders opened up a school here in Texas, but it closed after only a few years. In 2001 Andre Agassi opened up an academy for at-risk kids like ours, but his was in Las Vegas, where he grew up. His started as a college prep school, and then like ours, he did a K-12, which actually closed in 2017 and was turned into a charter school called Democracy Prep. Robinson's academy, Carver, is more religious-based. It started out as a private school but is now a public charter school.

We knew Robinson's school in the beginning was going to struggle a bit because of what we'd been through building ours, even though the focus of our schools are totally different. He was on the eastside of San Antonio, and they were dealing with more private money, and when hard times hit and the economy goes bad, people can't really afford private schools the way they used to. Then Robinson joined the IDEA Charter School Management Company, which has probably 50,000 students under their umbrella. It's the biggest charter school system in Texas, and things got better for his school. But our charter school may be the only one left of those first 20 in Texas.

The NBA used to hear about my program. They always used to highlight Robinson's great school, even though my school had a long history of nothing but success. But Charlie Rosenzweig, senior vice president of entertainment and marketing at NBA Entertainment, took time and really looked to see what we were doing with my schools. He was flabbergasted. He said, "George, I just thought you had a program that was in a strip mall or something."

And I said, "Well, you know I don't market it because that's not my purpose. I'm not doing this to tell people what I'm doing." But I'm also not stopping anyone from finding out on their own. We had a lot of success, averaging around 1,400 to 1,500 students a year. We had a budget of $15 to $16 million a year, we had 250 to 260 employees, and a good board of directors. I never wanted the attention. Once they see you're on top, somebody is always going to want to take you down. That was our motto. Plus, I wasn't doing it for the acclaim. I didn't build the schools for the attention; we built them to provide opportunities.

I'm grateful because there's a great need. It's giving back and never leaving a community that embraced me and one that I've chosen to make my home. I stayed in San Antonio. I saw the need for underserved kids educationally who weren't getting what they needed through the public school system here. Our enrollment is 51 percent Hispanic and 46 perceent African American, and then other ethnicities make up the remaining 3 percent. Ours is for the less fortunate. Not long ago we looked at our history to see how much we've been able to generate as far as government money we've received. We found out that we brought in more than $300 million to this community since our inception of the first youth center. We've graduated thousands of kids. We've had kids graduate from our school, graduate from college, come back, and bring their kids to our schools. It's created generational educational opportunities so that we grow our learners. It's an unbelievable history of community service, and that's what I really want to be known for. For helping people. That's what I'd like for my legacy to be. Some want theirs to be championships and rings. I don't have anything against that. Everybody has their own thing, but that's secondary to me.

* * *

My heart was crushed, too. When I heard about the babies, those kids at Robb Elementary School in Uvalde, Texas. I've been to Uvalde. It's only an hour and a half away from me. It probably hit me different than most not only because Uvalde is so close to us, but also because it's kids and it was a school, and I'm very closely connected to and invested in both.

We have security guards at our schools. *Armed* security guards in place to stop a negative force that comes to harm our kids. They walk around all day during school while the kids are there because I know it can happen. It can happen to our schools the same way it has to these other schools. We talk about it all of the time. We talk about gun laws and gun ownership and gun rights and how we need to get rid of this gun and that gun, but as someone whose name is on several schools that has thousands of kids in them, I only look at the fact that these children are our future jewels. If you have security cameras and armed guards protecting diamonds and pearls and gold because they are jewelry and because they have value, then our kids deserve the same protection. That's why I call them jewels.

The guns aren't going anywhere. I don't care whatever kind of laws our government passes; the guns are going to be here. The bad guy or the sick guy is always going to be able to get a gun. And he or she is not going to give up their guns. They got them illegally so what are they going to give 'em back for? There are so many guns. There are actually twice as many guns in this country as people at this point. They're ingrained in our society. They can take away all of the assault weapons, and it won't do anything. It's not going to work. But what we can do is do what's necessary to protect our children. My philosophy for our schools is to put up a deterrence because unfortunately sick people like soft targets. They're cowards in that sense. They're like snakes. They wait and sit and hide in the bushes and then sneak in to get you. They're ambushers. And unfortunately that's the reality we live in, and too often those soft targets happen to be our schools. The other reality is mental health remains something we do not address enough. We know all of these things that can occur. So why don't we put in place protection so that those types things don't happen? Even with all of the years of proof we have that it can happen at schools, there's still nothing in place.

We probably should have every door covered to the point where if something like Uvalde happens again, they won't pass. They won't be able to stay in one area without being confronted with the same malice they had when they entered our school. We can talk all day about the particulars of what happened, about the police standing out there, and what they did and did not do, but those are all just stories. Let's talk about prevention. Let's talk about this *not* happening. When the planes got hijacked, they put up secure doors on the planes so that you can't get in the cockpit. They put prevention in place because they were guarding what they felt was valuable. They were doing anything to avoid the same thing from happening again. How valuable are these babies who we are raising, who we are educating in our society? From the looks of things and because these same atrocities keep happening at these schools, I'll say: very little. And that's me as an administrator in education exposing the system that we live in. We ain't doing enough to protect our babies. Now who's going to stand up?

I think if you sit 100 people down and ask them what they want out of life, 99 and a half of them will say they want a peaceful environment. And we don't have that here. Not on this Earth. Everything is rat-a-tat-tat. Life is tough for a lot of people. I'm fortunate to the point that I don't have to deal with a lot of the pain and suffering that so many others in life have to, but that doesn't keep me from being concerned. My momma said all of the time, "Misery loves company." And the only way you can beat that is with love. The greatest protection we have is to display love for others. And it's hard to love others if we first don't love ourselves.

CHAPTER TWENTY

THE PEOPLE

A good name is better than gold.

I presented Hugh Evans into the Basketball Hall of Fame in 2022. Reggie Miller did it with me. Think about that: a ref. How many players present referees into the Halls of Fame? Can't be many. That tells you a lot about people.

I was the type of player, type of guy, where I had my own relationships with the refs. I always respected them whether they were bad or good. Didn't make a difference. I always had the understanding and played with the understanding that they weren't good sometimes. And that's what's important: *sometimes*. They made wrong calls sometimes; they make mistakes sometimes. So I always looked at it and what they did as a whole and kept that in relation to what I was doing. I made bad plays *sometimes*, I took bad shots *sometimes*, I made mistakes and make bad choices *sometimes*. Looking at it like that, I realized the most important thing I could do while I was playing with a referee was to respect him. I never had a problem with them. I kinda joke about my own way of co-existing with them. So I had my own way of communicating with them. "Get him off me, ref!" I'd say that every time I went to the hole. And I had the ball a lot. Think about it. I averaged 30 points. I said "Get him off me" so much they knew I wasn't telling them what to do, but that was my way of having fun with them. Just talking to them. Saying things like, "And one" with a smile on my face when I scored. It didn't matter if I was fouled or not. I think the referees enjoyed it. More importantly, I think they understood it. And if they understood I wasn't going to embarrass them, they respected me back.

In my whole pro career, I got thrown out of one game. To me—and this might be where it comes down to dealing with people or maybe it goes back to that "cool" thing that everyone tries to say is just a part of my personality—you can't lose yourself to a point where you get so upset you can't control yourself, and someone has to throw you out. Not as a player. I let that happen once, never again. Now I can see where sometimes a coach does it, but that's strategy. They're trying to change the momentum of the game, trying to get the team riled up, or trying to get the players emotionally into it. So they'll go after a ref, get thrown out, maybe that will uplift the team. But as a player, I knew there could be a chance where a ref could make a bad call and cost us a game. I played with that understanding. But at the same time, I could miss a shot or make a turnover that could cost us the game. That made us even.

I wish Evans would have been alive for his induction. He passed away only two months before he went in. When his wife Cathy called me, she said, "Ice, Hugh wanted to ask you himself to present for him at the Hall of Fame, but he was too weak to call you."

All I said was, "I'll be there." One of the more humbling and personal honors I've received was doing that. And for a referee to ask a ballplayer...wow.

* * *

People say I came from nothing, but I really come from a lot. I had an unbelievable mother who showed me how love works by showing me love and telling me she loved me. Same with Willie Merriweather, same with Dr. Robert Sims. And so many others. They taught me how to appreciate people. And I've lived my life trying to do just that: appreciate people and the relationships I've been fortunate enough to have with them. Some say money makes the world go around, but for me people make the world go around.

Toward the end of finishing this book, someone asked me if reliving my life and doing all of the reflecting changed me in anyway. Because often when people retell their life stories, they learn something about themselves they never knew. Well, over the last few years, I've gotten the chance to hear some of the people I've intertwined with through my career and in life speak about me, and to hear them speak of me in the ways that they have is very humbling. To say the least. Because I never took it or them for granted. After hearing them I reflected on the journey I've been on, and it's obviously a redemption story.

It's touching. Especially when it comes to my family because I could have lost them back in those dark times. For the documentary I didn't have my family do any rehearsing, none. I told them: "Just talk to 'em." And with them being open and honest with the filmmakers, you could just see how they loved me and how they guarded and protected me. It was a display of love. Love that they have for me but also the love that they know I have for them. I saw how they chose their words. Because they don't do these things. They don't get on camera, speak to the media. That ain't what they do. That can be intimidating. But I loved watching my wife, Joyce. Because she's been through it all, took the burnt of the good and the bad times with me. I just love how she took those deep breathes when speaking about our lives and how she guarded her words while telling our truths. Protecting her husband. She ain't gonna let you say anything harmful about her husband and she definitely ain't gonna say anything harmful against her husband. Even got my grandson in there, which was important to me. There wouldn't have been a documentary if they weren't involved because they are so much involved in my life. The world sees you one way, and then your family sees you for everything you really are. They have to deal with the pressures and how the world treats you—and how you react to it.

* * *

Michael Ray Richardson and I talk a lot. We laugh about our lives today because both of us are on the other side. His drug addiction was more public than mine. He went through hell. That's why I have so much love and respect for him overcoming it. What he had to go through shows me how strong he really is. He'll never get the credit for his strength that he deserves as a human being. People will never look at it that way. They'll say about his addiction: "Well, he did it to himself. It can happen to anybody." Okay now, don't count yourself out because life has its own way of turning on you. And from one addict to another, seeing his recovery process is unbelievable.

I look at it sort of like the way I look at coaching or teaching to a degree. How can someone take you to the next level when they never ever been there? How is someone going to tell you about drugs and alcohol if they never ever been there? I had to get my own spiritual strength to even be able to talk about my situation. But that's the influential part. I can dig down and be helpful to someone else. But the enemy don't want that; the enemy doesn't want you to help somebody else. But it's down there in all of us who have recovered. We just have to regurgitate it. We have to find a way to get it out of ourselves to help others. There's a brotherhood for those who are struggling with that disease. That's why I love to talk to the ones who are going through it. I like to make them laugh and think at the same time. That's really the joy of being human. The ability and possibility we all have to help someone else.

I saw Fatty Taylor when he was on his last leg. I went to Denver where he was living to see him. I saw him in the hospital in December of 2017 the same day they put him in hospice. I was here for a couple of days. One of our guys, Al Warren, he was there from the beginning and he told me, "Man, he was waiting on you." Because Fatty died the next day. He died when I was on my way back home.

That's what I needed for relief and closure. I was able in the end to spend that time with him. I always think about if I wouldn't have gone and he'd passed I would have missed something special and I'd be beating myself up, knowing that I could've just taken my time and gone to see him. But I didn't go to his funeral. I didn't go because I didn't want to. Because I'd *seen* him. Before he passed. I honored him the way I felt was the right way for what he and I had, the way I felt it was important to me. Now if I hadn't have seen him before that, I probably would have gone to his funeral. Said my good-byes to him there. I've always tried to respect that aspect of how going to a service is more for the family. And even though I knew his family, I didn't want to intrude on that. I based my decision strictly on the relationship he and I had.

We had a 50th ABA reunion that the Dropping Dimes Foundation hosted in Indianapolis in April 2018, and that was the last time I saw Bird Averitt. He'd had a stroke and was in a wheelchair. Couldn't walk. It broke my heart because I remember him running around with me. Once he left San Antone, I didn't see him that much anymore. I'd only seen him a few times because he ended up going back to Kentucky. And like everything else, life has its own way of dealing with you. But when I saw him, I treated him like he'd never had a stroke and like he was still walking. We had fun. I got a chance to tell him that I loved him and that I missed him.

Averitt was with me when I was trying to climb that ladder. He helped me climb that ladder, and I wanted him to know that I didn't go that far past him. He ended up passing two years later. But we had that time at that reunion. That's where we celebrated. I always wanted my guys, who had misfortunes, to know that I'd never forget them. That was always important to me. I wanted to do whatever I could do to still make them feel good and let them know that the relationship that we had still made me feel good. I tried to never lose sight of that. Giving these brothas their flowers while they can smell 'em.

The other life philosophy I've tried to live by beside the one my mother instilled in me is that it's our responsibility as older men to teach younger men to be better men. I've always wanted to help young men try to take the right steps to prolong their life, careers, or relationships, whatever. I never envied anyone, never cared what anyone else had or got, never cared about fame or fortune, never cared if someone got more money than I did or if their contract was bigger than mine. What I did care about was if you were making some bad choices or talking some bad steps, and if I can have some influence to help you get back on track, that's what I'm going to do. That's a passion of mine. And doing that has never been a big deal to me because that was just a part of my makeup, so when I hear that I'm beloved and I hear that I've been an influence on people, that means what I've set out to do worked. It's just a beautiful thing when you hear that from someone else.

That's the beauty of it. I'm trying to help these young men not make the same mistakes I made. If I haven't walked it, I can't tell anybody how not to walk it. They won't listen to you if you haven't. And I like to have fun talking to young men, especially youngsters. I can talk to youngsters, and their mouths drop open. They're always like, "Wow, that's me." And it is. I was them. I keep telling them: you all ain't gotta reinvent the wheel. We're just fixing a flat.

Is this the NBA's responsibility to talk to these kids? I say no. Is it the National Basketball Players Association's responsibility? I say yes. Two separate things. The owner's job in the NBA is to make money. We know how corporate America is. It's about that bottom dollar line. But the Players Association? It should be about the players' well-being and to teach them how to keep earning those dollars. A lot of players lose all of that because they don't have any structure, they don't have anyone to talk to. Really talk to. Like even though that investment property deal I made ended up in court, I'd tell the players about the experience and the reason I did it. When I was playing, I used it as a write-off, and once I retired, my plan was to use it as income. And that's where I'd like a large part of my legacy to rest: in the minds and futures of these young men playing the game today. You hear so many stories about these guys losing hundreds of millions of dollars, and I hate it when people talk bad about them losing $100 million or whatever.

First thing: that $100 million was never $100 million. They're at a 35 percent tax bracket. But with so many of us not being educated about money, players too often spend it like it's $100 million. They didn't remember that ol' 35 percent Uncle Sam's gonna get. And if Uncle Sam don't get it off the top, that 35 percent turns into 65 percent, then 75 percent. And that's what kills them. Too many don't have an understanding of that. How could they? Especially when they're not talking to or given access to talk with the guys who've been through it. They're coming into this game as corporations and don't even know it. Their whole lives change the second they sign that paper, and if they don't know it, they are going to lose it. They're going to keep living the only lifestyle they knew coming up: hanging out with the boys, spending money, having fun. Living for today, never thinking about tomorrow. And before they know it, today becomes five years, six years, eight years. That quick. Look up and you got nothin'. Bought their mom and them a big ol' house. After they pay for it, they ain't got the same money or any money, and now she can't take care of it. They get a million-dollar house in a beautiful place, but the property taxes are $50,000 extra a year. Where's that money going to come from? And without that knowledge and that kind of proper teaching, how are they going to understand?

The league has its little programs and things, but those are monitored. I didn't ever want to be a part of them because of that. I always tell them the same thing I told myself when I was young: "You got two ways you can do your 1–12. You can do your 1-12 in an educational facility, or you're going to do your 1–12 in jail." It's that simple. They've got to know the fundamentals of the system they are living in because without it they don't know the rules for survival. These NBA programs are teaching these kids how to make money from them. They're not teaching them how to make money for themselves and generational money for their families. They're not teaching the fundamentals of how to become wealthy. They're teaching them how to get that orange and squeeze all of the juice out of it that they can, and once it's dry, they put you out to pasture. Now you gotta go get your own juice. And nobody's taught you how.

And I'm not mad at them, I'm not mad at the league because ultimately that's not its job. It's not doing anything against the players; it's just not doing everything for them. But that's why we have a union, a players association. That's why I put it all on the union. The union makes enough money where it can create a system where the players gotta go through it to get this knowledge, make it so they don't have a choice. Protect the long-term assets and aspects of their lives. Just based on the fact that there's been so many before them who've gotten lost and lost everything because they didn't have a system in place. Think about it: a guy who makes $100 million should never be broke again in his life. Never. We should have something in place where we as former players should be able to educate these guys. Tell them how that fee of the agent, who negotiated that contract, is a part of that $28 million not that $40 million. They don't have that understanding, and before they know it, they're broke. And then they fall into depression. Then they turn to things like drugs and alcohol to deal with that, to dull that pain, which has now become a mental health problem. Or they hit or physically abuse their girlfriend or wife to dull the pain that they're carrying inside about themselves. Now they've become emotional wrecks. Sometimes for the rest of their lives. All because no one taught them where they were going and how to handle it when they got there. It's our responsibility as older men to teach younger men to be better men. You can do it silently; sometimes you do it by example. But when it's all said and done, that's our job. That's the purpose I serve.

When you fight evil with evil, it seems like you're at a spot where you have to keep fighting all of the time. So I learned you gotta instill your own love. I've always tried to teach or give advice with a sense of compassion. I've never been one to force my thoughts, feelings, or beliefs on anyone. I'm not the kind of guy, who's going to tell someone I try to help, to do what I tell you. I don't do things to receive credit or any type of acknowledgment for doing them. I do things out of virtue to help others when I can. That's all. Now if they want to tell others about our experience or that I helped out a bit, that's on them. But I ain't going to promote it.

I've had a lot of young pro players who've come through me, who I've spent time with, who came to spend a couple of days with me. From Stephon Marbury to Jason Terry to

Tobias Harris and more recently Emoni Bates. All I do is tell them, "This is what you all need to be on." But the difference is they didn't grow up doing it. By the time they get to me, they've already implemented the way they play into their everyday routines and development, so it's hard to change. At that point it's usually too hard to implement those new things that I'm trying to give them into their games. And even when those things are applied, once things get tight in a game, they go back to what they know—not what they just learned. I always say under stress people go back to their old habits. I see it all of the time. I laugh, though, every time I see Marbury. I showed him how to really get his jump shot off the ground. And when I showed him, he freaked out. He said, "I didn't know this. I never knew this."

I said, "That's because no one ever showed you." And all I'm doing is sharing with them, something I've been doing since the beginning. And while what I'm sharing with them is about basketball, more than anything what I'm really talking to them is about character. You always wonder what level of influence you really had on a person. Take someone like Tobias, who I've known all of his life because I've known his father, Torrel, since Torrel was 15 years old and I've watched he and his wife raise a beautiful family.

When Tobias was looking to purchase a house, he said, "I want one like you got, where you out there by yourself." And what he was talking about was the serenity. And even as a young man at the age that he was at the time, he knew that's what he wanted out of his life. That's what we all want. We all want to be around peaceful surroundings. Especially after doing what we do for our lives for the amount of time we do it in our lives. And for me to hear that from Tobias was so good to hear because it made me feel that he was able to see a part of my life up close. Made me feel that I had some small influence on him as a whole. Not as just a basketball player but as a whole person.

I believe a big part of the beloved feelings people have for me also comes from the way I try to treat situations, not just people. Take Nike. We've done some great things and had some great moments together, but I'm sure the main reason they kept putting me in those commercials was because I was always talking to people on the sets, telling stories, making them laugh, sharing moments, and because I was always fair with them as a company. That's how we built our relationship. I never had an agent when it came to do deals with them. Mark Thomashow would always tell me, "George, I spent my whole life dealing with talent agents, music labels, NBA agents, coaches, agents, lawyers, and you were the most enjoyable negotiator I've ever dealt with."

I always kept things simple. They'd ask me how much I wanted to be in a certain commercial, and I'd ask, "What do you all think is fair?" They'd say a price, and as long as I thought that was fair, I'd say, "Let's do it." And I know that's a big part of why I've been in so many of those Nike commercials. It wasn't because I was cheap, or that they didn't have to pay me a lot of money. It was because I was fair, and even when it came to negotiating, I treated them the way I wanted them to treat me.

It all reminds me of Willie Merriweather and Doc Sims. They ain't ever want anything from me, but what they always said was: "What you learn from me from the things that I'm able to give you and show you, give to somebody else." That became a part of me. So if I can help anyone become better, I do. Or I try. One of the most beautiful things I've learned in my journey is that a good name is better than gold in this life. Better than silver. Platinum. Diamonds. When somebody trusts you, you're there. When people have that kind of trust in you as a human being, ain't nothing greater. Nothin' greater in the world. I want to have that with people.

At the Hall of Fame inductions in 2022, I was with Bob McAdoo, and 'Doo said, "Ice's the one I passed the baton to for scoring." Now he won three scoring titles in a row from 1974 to 1976, and then Pete Maravich won his in '77, and then I took over beginning in '78.

So when 'Doo said that, I said, "You better believe it. Ain't no doubt about that." I couldn't help but admire his ability to put that ball in the hole. So when he did pass that baton, all I had to say was, "I'll take it from here."

There's that narrarive, the one that's put out there now against players who've never won a championship. My grandson hears all of these players' names and doesn't hear my name mentioned and says, "Well, Granddad" almost like he's feeling sorry for me. It makes me laugh because he doesn't know that that's what they are pushing, not necessarily the whole story of me or the whole truth. And as long as he loves me, I don't care nothin' about a career.

I tell him, "As long as you and I have that love for one another, I don't care nothing about that ball. And you'll see. Because that ball is only part of my story."

Life is a gradual process. The hope is that we're all working toward finding that peace in our lives. When you walk into our kitchen, one of the first things you'll see is a decorative sign by the stove that says: "Walk by faith, Not by sight." I try to live by that every day. I've had an unbelievable life, but I know so many people who've suffered and still are, and they just don't have any hope. I want to help give those people hope. Let them know better days are coming. At the NBA 75 celebration, I was asked, "Ice, what do you want to be recognized for, man?"

I said, "I want to be recognized as a helper of people."

EXODUS

Ain't no hearsay; it's he say.

I'm at peace with myself.

That's a major reason I decided to do this book. I wanted to talk in my own words and tell my story in a way that everyone could get to know George, not Ice. Because my story is about caring for more than just myself. From my own experiences and things I've gone through, I don't want to do anything but help somebody else understand how important it is to have spirituality and show love to people and to conquer hate. All the little things that we thought was nothing really mean the most. All of the guys and girls, who are controlled by something—whatever it is—you gotta find yourself out of that hole. All of those dealing with mental health issues, get the help you need. Who's your somebody? Find your *somebody*.

The one thing I am still learning to be at peace with is my last All-Star Game in 1985. It's strange. Michael Jordan was a rookie. And they have this narrative out there that Isiah Thomas, Magic Johnson, and I plotted against Jordan to make him look bad. And that's so insulting to me. But whoever put it out there, it worked. Because he believes it, and it hurts me that he does. For one thing: at the time I was a 13-year vet. I knew my time was coming to an end, even though I knew I still could play. Because Jordan was getting a lot of pub, I'll never forget in the West locker room of that All-Star Game in Indianapolis that the media came up to me and said, "Hey, Ice, Ice, tell us this: what does it feel like playing against that rookie Michael Jordan?"

I said, "Hey wait a minute! You need to go ask Mike what it's like playing against Ice," and then laughed. And they got up from there and obviously they must've gone over to the East locker room and told Jordan. And then I hear this narrative, which doesn't even make sense. *I was playing against him! How would I have frozen somebody out from the other side?* And I didn't hang with Magic and Thomas like that. Different generations. Who gonna bring something up like this—and include me in it? Then I read Charles Oakley's book and I'm all in his book talking about that from when I came to the Chicago Bulls the following year. Oak was a rookie that year and he obviously heard something from someone because it's in the book, but he sure doesn't know what he's talking about on this matter. I didn't do anything to disrespect Jordan but to try and blow him up by scoring on the other end and guard him on defense because I'm still a pro, a vet, and a competitor.

Oak said in his book, "Ice was going at him." Well, I went at everybody. If someone came out of the stands, I was going to go at them. If anyone reading this book was guarding me,

I'd go at them. But I never understood how I got thrown into that situation against Jordan. It's something I never addressed with anybody. Never talked about it with Jordan. Even when we played with each other in Chicago the next year, I didn't feel a need to because I didn't do anything. And that's the first thing the media said when I came to Chicago: "Well, Ice, what are you going to say to Michael?"

I said, "I'm going to say the same thing I always do: 'Wassup.' What do you think I'm gonna say?"

In his Hall of Fame speech, Jordan even mentioned it. He said, "Gervin." And that made me want to go up there—because I was sitting pretty close to the front—and tell him, "Hey, Mike, I ain't have nothing against you, never did anything against you." I'm also from Detroit so I also wanted to kid him and say, "Hey, listen here, m-----f-----, man what you talkin'?"

But obviously back then in '85, I was grown, and there are things you just let go by, and later that next season, I went to Chicago to play, and he got hurt. Then he had to watch me for 35 games. I was older then, but I still had some flashes of the Ice of old. We didn't go far, even though we made the playoffs, and that was when Jordan came back and put up that 63 against the Boston Celtics. Even though we didn't get to know one another then, I enjoyed my time with him because I was able to see him in the beginning of what turned out to be a more-than-special career. And knowing how narratives can be put to work, I knew one day I'd have a chance to tell my story, which is why I never felt the need to fight it, dispute it, or say it wasn't true. All these years I've listened to people make all of these stories up or make comments like, "Gervin and them were jealous of Mike."

I ain't ever been jealous of Jordan, never had any reason to be. I'm real, real comfortable and confident in the career that I had. And thankful for it. I never looked at what somebody else was doing, what somebody else was getting, how they were living. That never was a part of me. I was always just thankful for the career I had and what I was able to get out of it—and that's a beautiful life. I had my turn. Now I want to get out of the way so that someone else can come through. I ain't say anything, wasn't a part of it. This is what I would tell Jordan: "I never was a part of anything like that toward you. I never would be because I never did anything but respect you, loved how you approached that game, and really loved the career that you had." People can say what they want, but that's the truth. And I still to this day hate that it sounds like Jordan believes this crazy conspiracy theory.

He and I did a video together for some TV show Jordan was hosting called "Greatest Sports Legends." We were at the Omni La Costa Resort & Spa in San Diego in 1987 right after I'd returned from Italy and I retired from the NBA, and that was the first time he and I really gotta chance to talk. They had us on an outside court, shooting around. That time I had on jeans while I was shooting. We laughed and smiled. It was so beautiful. It was just really me and him. That's the relationship I know he and I really could have had. Something special. How we talked, how we interacted, how I could put a smile on his face. I think that was the first time he really saw me for me.

And then to see what he said about me in my documentary, it warmed my heart. I was delighted to hear that a man, who grew to the caliber of Jordan, can show that kind of humility and be able to talk about somebody before him. He said if he and I could have hooked up together when I was younger, "We would have been two bad m-----f------." And he said it with passion. He recognized. But for me it was *how* he said it that got to me. He said it with so much respect. And if you know Jordan, he likes joking with you, but on this he was very serious. He spoke about me with so much love. I tell my wife, "I love you" and at the same time I can tell my guys, "Man, I love ya." Those are different kinds of love, expressed in different ways.

Jordan kept going back to that one game. He said, "George had had his turn. And he knew it. He had that one more time to show his greatness." As confident as I am about what

I was able to do on that court, I never looked at myself as a bad m-----f-----. But after hearing what Jordan said about me, I felt like a was a bad this and a bad that.

Now he's not from the era of the guys hooping today, but he's from an era after me, and they have more admiration for us than we know. And I never knew Jordan felt that way about me. He felt the way about me as I did after meeting Oscar Robertson. Or knowing Spencer Haywood. Or playing as a young man with Ralph Simpson. Jordan apparently had the same admiration about me. Was I shocked? No, I just found it rewarding because of the career he had, the success he's had. He's a lot more humble than I thought—or the way he makes us believe he is. And I think that's a loss for all of us to not know how humble he really is. We ain't seeing the real picture. How he played and who he is are two different people. And being able to express what he expressed and how he expressed it about me tells me that he really has compassion and humility. To help tell my story, he almost put the shield down.

When we were on the Bulls, he was on his journey, and mine was about to be over. And because of that, we didn't really form that communication. But I always observed him, and he always watched me. It's our responsibility as older men to teach younger men to be better men, and Jordan was younger than I was on the Bulls, so he falls into that category.

It made me believe that he was paying attention. More so now than before. For him to pull out things that I've done and accomplished, it was strictly out of love and respect and understanding the game. One comment he made was about when we played a game against the Dallas Mavericks, and I got 35 points in a half. He recognized that I was at the end of my career and ended the game with about 40. He said, "George could've had about 70 or 80, but he just got tired." He said I got "tired" not in a way to criticize. He meant that it was just that time in my career. He knew for me it was over and that he was about to take over.

And that's when I said to him before we left the court, "Well, young fella, I was just trying to show you how it used to be." And that's the beauty of both of us making strong statements of nothing but love.

I don't regret not saying anything to him about that whole '85 All-Star Game situation even now. And I don't wish that he'd said anything to me about it. I think things happen when they are supposed to. I think it's a time in our lives where we're both older, and we can appreciate things of this nature in our lives differently. It's more beneficial. Back then what I said—if I'd said something—it could have been twisted, I could have been emotional, and I could have said the wrong thing. Or I coulda said the right thing, and he might not have taken it right. It happened just the way it was supposed to because both of us are still here. We are both grown men, and our careers are over. We have different perspectives now on how we look at things like that. We've had time to think about things and what it meant to us and somebody else. And it's good when you are at this stage of your life because you can think about somebody else other than yourself. I think that's the beautiful part about it. So I also ain't mad at Oakley, but what I'm saying is what he's saying ain't true. I'm not ever going to confront him about it or anything. It don't mean that much to me. But this is my own book, and it has the truth. Ain't no hearsay; it's *he* say.

* * *

When you find out about His father and His heavenly son and how His son was, and He says: "I'm giving you an example." That's our guide. He was perfect; we are not. Even today He's still giving us an example to follow. If you understand that and try to apply it to your life, you'll see better things happen for you. I'm understanding that even more today as I get closer to my time ending. It seems like we always get closer to God once we get in our upper years. When we are younger, we're so influenced and so distracted with how the world perceives us and we're still trying to figure this whole thing out. But those values, morals, and principles again, that's that parenting from my mom, what she instilled in me, that I caught on to early, saved, and structured me. I know those are the keys to how you deal with life and how it comes at you. I was able to have an impact on people and now that I'm older I see that it was a positive impact. To be able to witness the impact that I've had on people over these years has been mostly positive brings joy to my heart. Because in the end—that's what life is all about.

I know I'm going to retire from the San Antonio Spurs organization sooner or later. It's been a long time, and there's been so many changes in ownership. So when I do walk away, I don't mind it being quiet. I'd rather be able to walk away from it as opposed to that other way. I had enough rah-rahs in my life. I'm settled, man. I just want to stay around long enough to play golf with my grandkids, show them how to hunt, knock down some of these deer I have out here. All of that type of stuff. It's small stuff to other people, but it's big to me. That's all I need. And at some point, I want to get back to Italy.

ACKNOWLEDGMENTS

If you've read this book, then you already know the first acknowledgment goes to the one I call Jehovah.

To my wife, Joyce, and our family. Our kids and grandbabies and great grandbabies whenever they get here.

To my mom. To my sisters and brothers.

To Merriweather and Doc Sims.

To the city of Detroit for giving me a foundation. To the city of San Antonio for giving us a place to call home.

As for the title, the original suggested title for the book was *Ice Never Melts*.

I responded in an email to my business partner, the coauthor, and Triumph Books: "*Born to Score* is what I like and this is why. That's what I was really known for. *Ice Never Melts* is cool, but I did melt. *Born to Score* you can and will see throughout the book. What I mean: recovery. I score with my school. I score from its success. Retirement homes for low income people, I score. We created jobs for people, I score. Over 27 in 30 years we brought into the San Antonio community, over 300 million for services education jobs, I score."

We ended up incorporating that as the subtitle and using part of my nickname *Ice* as the main title because Triumph Books said how cool that was.

As Scoop and I talked, I never thought I was cool. Scoop really helped me understand how people perceived me. But me, myself, I was and am always just trying to be me.

Because in the end I wanted this book to be more about life, not just my life. Lessons I've learned, lessons we can all carry with us while we're here. That's the hope I have that this book leaves you with.